THE TOTAL PACKAGE

The Balanced Life

DENNIS L TAYLOR

Copyright © 2022 Dennis L Taylor

All rights reserved. No part of this book may be used or reproduced by any means, graphic, electronic, or mechanical, including photocopying, recording, taping, or by any information storage retrieval system without the written permission of the publisher except in the case of brief quotations embodied in critical articles and reviews.

Scriptures are taken from the New International Version of the Bible

Books may be ordered through booksellers or by contacting:
Dennis Taylor
luke252.dennis@gmail.com

Raising The Standard International Publishing L.L.C.

ISBN: 978-1-955830-76-8
Printed in the United States of America
1st Edition Date: August 2022

Dedication and Thanks

I want to dedicate this book, "The Total Package," to the memory of two very special people in my family. Both family members were what I would call a total package in Christ. They both left this world way too early, but God saw it fit to take them both on to heaven to be with Him. They were truly loved and adored by many.

I first want to honor the life of Debbie Durham from Moultrie, Georgia. She was my sister-n-law and was married to David "Bull" Durham. Debbie was considered a saint by many people, and she was one of the most patient people who ever walked the face of this earth. She was kind, loving, and considerate, and she was such a compassionate person, and she always put other people's needs in front of her own. Debbie was also a God-fearing mother who always gave Jesus first place in her life. She lived out her faith daily and loved the people around her well. Debbie had a battle with cancer and passed away on December 3, 2018. She lived a life that made Jesus smile.

Danny Durham is the second person I would like to honor with this book. Danny never met a stranger. He would strike up a conversation with anyone and make them feel like they had been lifelong friends. Danny enjoyed life and also loved making people laugh. He had a contagious personality and loved to tell a good story. Danny knew how to draw you in and keep your attention. He played football at Georgia Southern under the leadership of Erk Russell and won two National Championship as a player. Danny went on to be a Graduate Assistant and won two more National Championships as a coach. From there, he coached high school football, married Julie Griggs, and began raising a family. Danny and Julie had three kids and ended up at Harris County High School, where Danny served as athletic director and vice principal. On August 16th, 2018, Danny was out on his daily run and collapsed. He passed away due to heart issues and left a huge hole in that school system. Danny touched many students' lives and made a difference in that entire county. He was the total package and a great man of God.

I also want to thank Carol Eilers for taking the time to edit this book. You are an amazing woman of God and loved by many. Not only did you read through this book several times, but you also prayed over it with love. That means the world to me. I could never say thank you enough or do anything to pay you back. Thank you for your patience and willingness to put up with me during this process. I pray God's greatest blessings on you and your ministry.

Thank you, Charles Morris and RSI Publishing. (Raising the Standard International Publishing L.L.C.) You have taught me so much in such a short period. Thank you for all the time and energy that you have invested in me and my two books. You are indeed a blessing to me and my ministry. "Thank you, Lord, for the gifts of a friend."

My final thanks go out to David Avelar for a beautiful front cover. You are only a senior in high school, and yet it is evident God has great things for you. Stay faithful, and keep using your skills for the glory of God.

Table of Contents

	Introduction	1
SECTION 1	*Jesus Grew In Wisdom*	5
Chapter 1	Ask For It	6
Chapter 2	Be A Continuous Learner	12
Chapter 3	A Continual Flow	20
Chapter 4	Surround Yourself With Godly Influences	26
SECTION 2	*Jesus Grew In Stature*	33
Chapter 5	Getting To The Starting Line	34
Chapter 6	Little By Little	39
Chapter 7	Setting Goals / Accountability	44
Chapter 8	Not A Diet	50
SECTION 3	*Jesus Grew In Favor With God*	55
Chapter 9	Break Down The Walls	56
Chapter 10	Build A Strong Foundation	62
Chapter 11	Build On It	66
Chapter 12	Open God's Love Letter	75
Chapter 13	Accountability	82
Chapter 14	March Down The Field	87
SECTION 4	*Jesus Grew In Favor With Man*	93
Chapter 15	Relationships	94

Chapter 16	Choose Your Words Wisely	102
Chapter 17	Put Love Into Action	111
Chapter 18	The Constant Pursuit	121
	More Books By Dennis Taylor	127
	About the Author	129

THE TOTAL PACKAGE

Introduction
Luke 2:52

Life can be so hard, and hard times will hit us from every side. In the real world, there are no timeouts, unlike in a football game. In a football game, if you are running out of time, need to make a quick decision about your next play, and are unsure what to do, you call a timeout. Don't you wish you could call a timeout when you are tired or when life gets hard? Life doesn't stop when things get hard or don't go as planned. I want to start by asking you a couple of questions and encourage you to think about these questions before you respond. Do you have lost dreams, or maybe you have experienced disappointments in life? Have you ever wondered what if? Does your life seem as if it is spinning out of control and being turned upside down? I will be the first to tell you I am not perfect and have made some bad decisions. There are many times in my life that I wish I could go back in time and change a few things like poor decisions, lack of effort, or even laziness.

However, we can't live life looking backward. We must keep moving forward with a positive attitude, facing obstacles, and climbing over them. Life should be about hitting hard times but not turning back or quitting. I struggled early in my life with that. If things didn't go my way, I would give up and quit. When something wasn't easy, or I had to face adversity, instead of stepping up or meeting the challenge, I found it a lot easier to quit or attempt to blame someone else.

I also struggled with balance and inconsistency in my life. I could do one thing and do it well, while other areas of my life fell apart. I know I am not alone. There are so many who struggle with this and continue to do the same thing over and over. Luke 2:52 has changed my life, and I want to share it now with you.

Luke 2:52 says, "Jesus grew in wisdom and stature, and in favor with God and man."

Jesus grew in every area of life. He grew physically, mentally, spiritually, and relationally. Jesus had a balanced life and is our ultimate example of how to live life. He is the total package. Therefore, we can say we are meant to grow in wisdom and be continuous learners. We are called to take care of our earthly temple by eating right, exercising, and using our energy to glorify God in everything we do. We were all created to draw close to God, enjoy His fellowship, and worship Him with all our might. Yes, to be like Jesus, we are to guard our relationship and deal with people in a way that will honor Him. We cannot be satisfied and content. It is easy to fall into a rut in life and feel sorry for yourself. Listen, it is time for a change. It's time to say, "I have had enough!" It's time to get started. What has happened to your dreams? Where is the passion for life? Have you quit yourself, your family, and even God? I know life can be overwhelming and challenging, but we must learn how to fight and never give up.

The good news is you don't have to do it alone. God has given you everything you need to win. If you are in Christ, He has given you the Holy Spirit. He is the One called alongside to help. The Holy Spirit of God lives inside of you. God hasn't given the spirit of fear but of power. The Lord also will bring other people around you that love you, care for you, and motivate you. It's time to return to your

THE TOTAL PACKAGE

first love. It starts with confession and spending time with the One who loves you the most. It's time to take care of the temple God has given you. Watch what you eat and how much you eat. Get your heart rate up and get off the couch. Don't be scared to try new things and even be willing to fail. I dare you to dream and, while you are dreaming, dream big. Finally, invest in relationships. For some, it's time to swallow pride and be willing to say I am sorry. For those who have been married for 20 years or more, it's time to take your wife on a date.

Think about it this way, most of our cars ride on four tires. Air pressures vary from car to car, but all four tires must have equal air pressure in all four tires to perform their best. Even when one tire's air pressure is low, it will cause issues when you don't correct the situation immediately. I have been guilty of ignoring the low tire pressure and made excuses for not stopping to correct the problem. I would say I don't have time or will do it tomorrow. But I would use the same excuse the next day too. Low air pressure or not having your tires properly balanced will cause your car to pull to the right or the left. It will also cause your tires to wear out faster than normal. That will cost you more money and more headaches. Then you start thinking, why didn't I slow down enough to get that tire right? Having your tires properly aligned and balanced may cost you a little more upfront, but your car will perform a lot better, and those tires will last a lot longer.

Is your life perfectly balanced and aligned with the Lord? Are you growing in wisdom and stature and favor with God and in favor with man? Is there a tire that is losing air? Is your life pulling to the right or the left? You may be like me, and you must slow down enough to look honestly at your life and your walk with the Lord. Pay attention to the warning lights of life and do something about it now. Jesus was balanced in every area of life. He is our ultimate example of how to live life. Be willing to follow the example that He set for us.

I can't wait to share what God has laid on my heart. I pray this book will challenge you and encourage you to make some positive changes in your life. Do not be pushed into the mold of this world.

1 Peter 1:13-15 says, "Prepare your minds for action; be self-controlled; set your hope fully on the grace to be given you when Jesus Christ is revealed. As obedient children do not conform to the evil desires you had when you lived in ignorance. But just as he who called you is holy, so be holy in all you do."

Prepare your mind for action. Be self-controlled. Do not be conformed to this world and what everybody else does around you but follow Christ's lead and the example He has given you. God has created you for greatness. You can do this. Live simple but dream big. My life is different, but I still have a way to go. We will all mess up and fall short sooner or later, but don't let that stop the pursuit of following the Lord, who is our perfect example of how to live life. We are called to be more and more like Christ every day. Dive in, and let's get started on "The Total Package."

Section 1
Jesus Grew
In Wisdom

Chapter 1
Ask For It

Luke 2:52 says, "Jesus grew in wisdom and stature, and in favor with God and man."

If I were to tell you today that I am about to share something that would change your life forever, and what I am about to share with you will make you a better parent, a better employee, and satisfied with life, would you want to find out what it was? Wouldn't you be sitting on the edge of your seat and listening closely to every word I speak? Well, here it is. Ask God for wisdom. Are you disappointed? Is there a huge letdown? So many times, we want a magical formula or a step-by-step process to the path to success. We want all the good stuff of life, and we want it now. I hate to tell you this, but growing in wisdom will not happen overnight, but it will come if we continually ask our Heavenly Father for it.

Jesus grew in wisdom. This was the most challenging section to write for me because wisdom is hard to come by or even understand. I believe retaining wisdom is a process; it takes time to gain it. In the story of Solomon in 1 Kings 2:9, David charges Solomon to be the new king over Israel and take the throne. Then David dies. In 1 Kings 2:10, Solomon begins his reign as King.

1 Kings 3:3 says, "Solomon showed his love for the Lord by walking according to the stature of his father David."

THE TOTAL PACKAGE

In 1 Kings 3:5, the Lord appeared to Solomon during the night in a dream. God said, "Ask whatever you want, and I will give it to you."

I don't know about you, but I would have had a mile-long wish list. So many things come to mind: money, fame, power, or just to be out of debt. Wouldn't it be great to know that you are debt free? I also long for a new, full-sized truck. I have a 2005 Chevrolet Colorado truck. It has over 200,000 miles, and not the first window will roll down. But it is paid for, and it runs so well. Solomon didn't hesitate; he knew what he wanted. Solomon was different from most of us.

In 1 Kings 3:9, Solomon answered God's question by saying, "Give your servant a discerning heart."

In other words, Solomon didn't ask for wealth, fame, and not even power. He asked for wisdom to govern his people, and his request pleased the Lord.

The Lord replied to Solomon in verse 10, "I will do what you ask. Not only will I give you a discerning heart but, I will give you riches and honor like no one has ever seen before."

The Lord continued his conversation with Solomon in 1 Kings 3:14:

"If you walk in obedience, I will give you a long life and riches."

Then Solomon woke up and realized that he was dreaming. What a crazy dream. Solomon's heart had to be racing, and his mind had to ask what had just happened. I can only imagine Solomon's excitement from this encounter with the living God.

1 Kings 4:29-34 tells us that God gave Solomon wisdom, great insight, and a breath of understanding as measureless as the sand on the seashore. The first thing we must grasp is that God gave wisdom to Solomon. Solomon didn't work for it, and he didn't earn it. God gave it to him as a gift. The second thing that jumps out to me is that God gave wisdom in abundance, as numerous as the sand on the seashore. I must admit I am not a huge beach fan, but my family loves it. So, I will follow along with my beach umbrella and sunscreen. Have you ever noticed when you go to the beach, you can never get all the sand off your body? The sand gets everywhere. I mean everywhere. Not only all over you, but in your car, your house, and it takes weeks to get it out of your shoes. As I sit under my umbrella drinking my cold water, my mind begins to wonder. How many grains of sand are there on this beach? I am sure there is a formula that someone can come up with to give you an accurate figure, but why waste our time? Let's just say there are so many grains of sand that it is almost impossible to count.

God blessed Solomon with incredible wisdom. 1 Kings 4:30 tells us Solomon's wisdom was greater than all the men in the East, greater than all the wisdom of Egypt, and he was wiser than any other man alive. Solomon spoke over 3000 proverbs and wrote 1005 songs. Try to wrap your mind around those figures! Men from all over the world would come just to listen to him speak and share his wisdom. Because of Solomon's great wisdom, God also blessed him with great wealth and favor.

You may be reading this and saying to yourself, "I am just an ordinary person, and there is nothing special about

THE TOTAL PACKAGE

me." I am with you, and I truly understand where you are coming from. I was lucky to graduate from high school. I would love to make a mark on this world and to make a difference in someone's life. Let me tell you something that will change your life forever. You can make a difference in this world! You can inspire others around you. This request for wisdom is where your new journey begins. Therefore, ask God for wisdom. It's time to go from existing to really living.

James 1:5 says, "If any of you lacks wisdom, he should ask God, who gives generously to all without finding fault, and it will be given to him."

Proverbs 2:6 says, "For the Lord gives wisdom and from his mouth comes knowledge and wisdom."

So, what are you waiting for? You see. God uses life experiences and people around you to teach you wisdom. The Word of God has plenty to say about wisdom. Look at a couple of verses in Proverbs with me.

Proverbs 3:13 says, "Blessed is the man who finds wisdom."

Proverbs 4:7 tell us, "Wisdom is supreme."

Proverbs 8:11 says, "Wisdom is more precious than rubies."

James 1:5 is one of the most powerful promises in God's Word. If God said it, you had better believe it. You can rely on the Word of the living God. He will never waiver, and He is never slack concerning His promises. God is faithful regarding His promises, but He rarely works on your timetable. Trust me on this one. How many of you can testify to that? I know you have heard that old saying, "Good things come to those who wait." It's like waiting for Thanksgiving dinner, and it is never easy. The turkey and ham are done and waiting to be cut, and the casseroles are about to pop out of the oven. Everything smells so good. You sit there and wait for the cooks of the family to say, "Come and get it." Will those words ever come? How much longer till we eat? Will it ever get here? It's coming, but you most likely will have to wait, but be patient and wait on the Lord. Here are a few more scriptures concerning wisdom.

Proverbs 23:23 says, "Buy the truth and do not sell it, get wisdom, discipline, and understanding."

Solomon himself is penning these words. Don't you think he knows what he is talking about? He received wisdom from God and experienced the blessing of walking in wisdom. I don't know about you, but if I wanted to learn how to cook, I would like to learn from someone who cooks every day. I want to learn from someone who has been cooking for a long time. I want to learn from someone who knows how to bring food alive, not someone who will just open a can of SpaghettiOs!

Solomon continues in Proverbs 29:3 and tells us, "A man who loves wisdom brings joy to his father."

As we close out the first chapter, here is my challenge to you: Go into a time of prayer with your Heavenly Father. Take time to get your heart right with him and be open and honest with Him. Get things straight and simply ask God for wisdom. Then open your heart, soul, and mind to what He will show you. I want to encourage you to hang on to James 1:5. Place it on your car's dashboard or the mirror in your

THE TOTAL PACKAGE

bathroom. Memorize it and pray this verse daily. Are you ready to receive it? Ask for wisdom. Don't forget that a loving father wants to give incredible gifts to his children. As an earthly father, I always wanted to provide more than what they expected for their birthdays and Christmas. I loved seeing their expression of being overwhelmed and surprised. If an earthly dad likes to bless their children and surprise them with blessings, how much more does the perfect Heavenly Father want to pour out outrageous gifts on His children?

Chapter 2
Be a Continuous Learner

Luke 2:52 says, "Jesus grew in wisdom and stature, and in favor with God and man."

I must be open and honest with you; I was never a great student. I had never read the first book in all my years of school. It is sad to say, but even the Cliff notes were too long for me to read. I saw schoolwork as something I had to do to play sports. I know. That is probably not a good thing to share, but that is God's truth. I would be delighted if I could make a B or a C. In 1985, I graduated from Dougherty High School in Albany, Georgia. Yes, I had a lot of good friends, but I was happy to move on with my life. I had a couple of offers to play football and baseball in college. To say the least, I was pretty much a homebody, and I had never been away from home. I liked being in my bed, eating my mama's cooking, and being around people who were familiar to me. Plus, my girlfriend, Laura Durham, was still in high school. She was the love of my life, the chosen one, and the apple of my eye. I signed with the closest school to my hometown of Albany, Georgia, but it was still two hours away from everything I loved.

In the fall of 1985, I showed up at South Georgia College to play baseball and take a few classes. Now I could pursue my dream of playing college ball and show the world how good I was. Up to this point in life, I was known as a good athlete that could throw a baseball 90 plus. I could throw down a 360 two-hand dunk on a good day and fling a football 65 yards. That fall, I began to practice with my new team. I was recruited to be a pitcher, so that meant that I would not be playing in the field. That was a rude awakening because I had always played the field when I was not pitching. College practice was different from practices in high school. If you were to pitch for Coach Stewart, you would be in great shape.

The practice became more like track practice than anything else. No more hanging out in the outfield, goofing off during batting practice. All the pitchers would run the foul poles repeatedly. We would go to left field, to the warning track, start at that foul pole, and hit a fast jog over to the right field foul pole. I remember thinking, this is not what I signed up for. If we weren't running foul poles, we were running laps around the field and stopping every so often to do pushups and sit-ups. Long story short, I left college and my baseball dream to pursue a career of making a lot of money. Watch out. Dennis Taylor is about to enter the business world.

I moved back in with my parents and ate at my mama's table again. I found a job that I was qualified for at Keenan Auto Parts. I was making a smooth $4.25 an hour. I wasn't sure what I would do with all that money. For the very first time in my life, I wasn't known for being an athlete. That may sound strange, but this was a significant transition in my life. I was the hired help. I loaded trucks, pulled parts, and swept the floors. It didn't take me long to realize I needed to do something else with my life. I remember thinking for the first time in my life; that I should have applied myself a little bit more when it came to schoolwork. I should have read that book and paid more attention in school. Up to this point, I had no desire to learn or better myself. I especially didn't want to read a book. Outside of the athletic realm, I was lost. Man, I had a bad case of regret. Have you ever been there? Regret has a way of stopping our forward motion.

We all have regrets in life. I don't care who you are. Even great men of God in the Old Testament found themselves full of shame, regretting decisions they made in the heat of passion. How about David, a man after God's own heart? He made a wrong decision when it came to Bathsheba! He fell into temptation and fell from grace.

Can you hear the regret in David's words in Psalm 51:1-4, "Have mercy on me, O God, according to your unfailing love; according to your great compassion blot out my transgressions. Wash away all my iniquity and cleanse me from my sin. For I know my transgression, and my sin is always before me. Against you, you only, have I sinned and done what is evil in your sight."

Now that is a man full of regret. How often do we look back on our lives and say we would love to have a do-over or wish we could go back and take advantage of learning from great teachers and coaches that we met all the way? One thing was for sure. I had to change how I viewed life. I had to grow up, and I had to start learning new things. I had to expand my horizons and find new dreams and passions. The Lord only knew how much my life was about to change.

I began to ask the Lord and myself so many questions. Like, what do I do with my life? How will I make a living? Where would I live? At the time, I didn't have a clue what God had in store for me to do. The great thing about it all is that God didn't reveal it all to me at once. As I began to ask for wisdom, He took His time and prepared me one step at a time. God gave me a passion for reading and studying. That was a miracle. He showed me how He could take my greatest fears and turn them into my greatest passions. He taught me to face and conquer difficult situations instead of running from them and hiding. Over time, God showed me the importance of not being content in life and how important it was to be a continuous learner.

Identify your regrets, loosen your grip, and trust God with them. Identifying your regrets isn't easy. If we were honest with ourselves, we spend so much time covering up our regrets while trying our best to erase them from our memory. But it is necessary to do if we want to grow in wisdom.

Philippians 3:13: "Brothers, I do not consider myself yet to have taken hold of it. But one I do: Forgetting what is behind and straining toward what is ahead."

There is another step to growing in wisdom, and it is having the guts to face our fears. One of my greatest fears in life was speaking in public. As a child, I hated when spelling bees would come around because I hated to say anything in front of other people. I didn't want people to make fun of me, and I especially didn't want to put myself in front of the class. I wasn't a good speller and was nervous in front of people. I remember misspelling a word in 2nd grade on purpose, just to be able to sit down and get back in my comfort zone. I also remember singing in a youth choir with 50 other friends at Sunnyside Baptist Church. I didn't mind choir practice because we had a great time and always had something to eat right after we finished. However, I had an issue when we had to sing at night during church in front of the whole church. But I had a plan. I would hold the choir booklet in front of my face and hide behind it. That is the only way I survived that terrifying experience. You would think I would overcome this crazy fear, but it worsened as I got older.

I will never forget my senior year of high school when I was voted President of the FCA. I thought it was cool, and I thought I could handle a small group setting once a week. I could call somebody to pray or invite my Youth Pastor to come and speak. No big deal, I could work all that out until I discovered all Club Presidents were asked to go to the auditorium. That morning we were going to welcome the upcoming 10th graders. What I didn't know was all Club Presidents had to stand up in front of everybody and tell them their name and what club they represented.

Are you kidding me? I didn't sign up for this. Right then and there, my heart began to speed up, my hands began to sweat, and I was looking for a way to escape. But before I could devise a plan to get out of there, the principal called me to stand up, introduce myself, and tell everybody what club I was representing. I remember thinking I could do this, and it wouldn't be that hard. Just stand up, do your thing, and sit back down. It took everything I had to stand up that day. I tried my best to speak, but I felt like someone had their hands around my throat. But I finally said, "My name is Dennis Taylor, and I am the President of FCA." I did it! My voice changed like five times, but I could sit back down. To my surprise, I didn't roll over and die. I survived. That was one of the most challenging things I had to do in high school, but it wouldn't be the last time I had to speak in front of a crowd.

Psalm 56:3-4: "The Lord is my light and my salvation-who shall I fear? The Lord is the stronghold of my life of whom shall I be afraid?"

THE TOTAL PACKAGE

I sit here today wondering how my life would be different if I had run out of that auditorium just to escape my greatest fear. It is amazing how God can take your greatest fear and turn it around to become one of your greatest passions. Today, there is nothing more exciting than standing in front of a crowd of people and sharing my heart with them. Being a continual learner isn't always easy. It will put you in spots where you will have to learn more about yourself that you don't want to know. It will take you into some uncharted waters and lead you to places where you will feel uncomfortable. But those things will lead you to growth and help you discover new passions and pursuits. Let me ask you some questions.

1. What are your regrets?
2. What are your fears?
3. What are your weaknesses?
4. How can you grow?
5. How can you overcome those insecurities?

1 John 4:16-18 tells us this, "God is love. Whoever lives in love lives in God, and God in him. In this way, love is made complete among us so that we will have confidence on the day of judgment, because in this world we are like him. There is no fear in love, but perfect love drives out fear, because fear has to do with punishment. The one who fears is not made in perfect love."

Perfect love drives out fear. If you were to be honest with yourself, some of these things have been with you for a long time. What is something you have always wanted to do in this life, but fear has always held you back? Fear is a liar, and it will keep you captive. It is easy to be caught up in mundane life. Don't let your life be about going to work, paying bills, and sleeping. Then wake up the following day just to do it all over again. Dare to commit to being a lifelong learner. Don't be scared to try something new and dare to dream. But when you dream, dream big because you serve a huge and mighty God.

I will be upfront and honest with you. Learning something new isn't always going to feel warm and fuzzy. There will be times when you stumble and fall. There will also be times of incredible frustration. Just know it is all a part of the process. It's God's way of teaching you how to think and pray things through. A continual learner learns how to deal with setbacks and develops a sense of creativity. I challenge you today to take your eyes off your regrets and fears and place them on God's love for you.

It is like having your first-born child. Laura, my wife, and I didn't have a clue how to raise a new baby girl. We read a couple of books and talked to many people about what to expect. Yes, we did make many mistakes along the way, and we were not perfect parents. There were some things I look back on today and wish I could go back and change or do it differently. Being a new parent is never easy. So many new challenges come your way with a whole new set of responsibilities, but being a dad changed my life forever. It caused me to grow up and taught me to be less selfish. I learned to put others before myself, which led me to love a little deeper. How about those nasty #2 diapers? They were the worst. Especially those diapers that couldn't contain all the content. I could have easily said, "I have never done this before. I don't know what to do."

As a first-time dad, I asked so many questions. I had so many fears and doubted my abilities as a parent. I didn't know how to be a good dad, but I jumped right in and learned. I had to learn a few new skills, and I had to learn how to trust my Heavenly Father with them.

We must ask God for wisdom and commit to becoming continuous learners to grow in that wisdom. That may look different to each of us, but I challenge you today to read. Reading and learning opened so many doors in my life. It is sad to say, but I didn't start reading till I was 20 years old. Then I discovered that I could learn from some of the godliest men and women in the world even though I had never seen them face-to-face. I was blown away by the enlightenment and the stimulation I received from reading. I entered a whole new world. I had to make reading a priority in my life. Therefore, I had to block out time to do it because of my busy schedule.

I want to challenge you to try new things and go and see new places. Get ready to see a whole new world and begin to dream. Let go of regret and don't hesitate to identify your fears, face them, and overcome them through the love of God.

John 16:12-13: "I have much more to say to you, more than you now bear. But when he, the Spirit of truth, comes, he will guide you into all truth. He will not speak on his own; he will speak only what he hears, and he will tell you what is yet to come."

Chapter 3
A Continual Flow

Luke 2:52 says, "Jesus grew in wisdom and stature, and in favor with God and man."

The older I am, the more I want to learn. I realize I have lived two-thirds of my life; realistically, I have only a few years left to live on this earth. That thought makes me stop and think. I don't know about you, but I love to do new things. I hate to get into a mundane routine. I have worked at AT&T for several years and am very grateful for my job. It has provided me with the means to support my family and to put my girls through college. I can say that I have met some brilliant people over the years and have enjoyed talking and learning from them all. The changes in technology are forever changing. With all the changes, sitting at a desk in an office for most of the day has become difficult. Yes, I have learned much about designing a fiber run or a GPON job for a new neighborhood. Even though there is a never-ending learning curve, designing for AT&T is not my passion. My passion is diving into God's Word. I can read His truth repeatedly and find new truths and realities every time. There is nothing more exciting than for God to open a door of new ideas on how to teach His Word. I love it when the Word of God jumps off the page and shows me a truth I need in my life.

There are so many things that come at you in this life. We all face times of hardship, tribulations, trials, and so many things that will rock your world. How about hearing the words, you have cancer? My mom plays a huge role in my life, and I will tell you upfront I am a mama's boy. I am not ashamed to tell the whole world. One day my mom noticed a knot in her gut area. Thank goodness she didn't push it off and think it was no big deal. She went to the doctor and found out the knot was ovarian cancer. Mom quickly underwent surgery, and the doctors successfully removed the growth, but they had to administer several radiation sessions. This sickness and treatments were tough for my mom and our family. But through it all, God's Word held her altogether. As her hair fell out and she was tired and hurting, she remained a woman after God's own heart. She was still kind and compassionate. She never once thought about herself and was more worried about how we were doing through all of this. God's Word was her strength; she trusted Him through it all. I learned more about the Word of God during this time of her life than I could have learned from a hundred sermons. Her life taught me about God's grace, His mercy, and His power to sustain us through difficult times as we trust Him. You see, it's not enough just to learn and to have the knowledge. You must be willing to share it and give it away.

Luke 6:39: "Give and it will be given to you. A good measure, pressed down, shaken together, and running over, will be poured out into your lap."

During those difficult times in mom's life, she shared her faith with me, whether she knew it or not. She shared wisdom with me as she walked out her faith in obedience. It is important to receive from the Lord, but it is just as important to share it with the people around you. Receiving and sharing create a continual flow in your soul, which is the difference between being healthy and being sick spiritually, physically, and emotionally. Let me illustrate for you.

The Sea of Galilee is a freshwater lake in Israel and is approximately 33 miles in circumference, 13 miles long, and eight miles wide. The maximum depth is 141 feet deep. It is also 186 feet below sea level. The lake is fed partly by an underground spring, although its primary source is the Jordan River, which flows through it north and south. Notice I said it flows through it. The Sea of Galilee has an inlet and an outlet. This body of water is a place where a South Georgia boy would love to go with a rod and a purple worm! It is beautiful, crystal-clear water, where the plant life is unbelievable.

But there is another body of water in Israel that is the opposite. Of course, I am talking about the Dead Sea. Like the Sea of Galilee, it is fed by the Jordan River, but the Dead Sea doesn't have an outlet. That is why the Dead Sea has a massive concentration of salt and other mineral deposits, and it is hard for vegetation and fish life to live there. To be healthy and to grow in wisdom, we need to have a constant flow of Christ in our lives.

Yes, we need to receive from the Lord. We require that steady, constant flow of God's goodness and wisdom, which comes by digging into God's Word. We receive by sitting under godly teachings and taking in truth. Yes, we also receive as we worship and meditate. But just like the Sea of Galilee, we need to have an outlet. We are not called just to gather information and take in sound knowledge and wisdom; we are also called to give it away. We are called to go and make disciples.

Matthew 28:18-20 Jesus said, "All authority in heaven and on earth has been given to me, Therefore go and make disciples of all the nations, baptizing them in the name of the

THE TOTAL PACKAGE

Father and of the Son and the Holy Spirit, and teaching them to obey everything I have commanded you, And surely I am with you always, to the very end of the age."

Those were Jesus' last words to us as a Church before He ascended to heaven. That is known as the Great Commission, not the Great Suggestion. It's not an option but a command from our Heavenly Father. We will become healthy and grow in wisdom as we receive from the Lord and learn to give it to others. As believers, we need God's constant steady flow in our lives.

Here is my challenge for you today. I want you to ask God for two things today: First, ask God to give you a hunger for His Word and the things of God. Growing up as a child, I was skinny as a rail. I ate my food, but mealtime was something I had to do as a child. As I aged, I wanted to put on some size, and I wanted to become stronger. So, I had to increase my calories. I had to start eating more and more food. I remember eating a full meal, forcing myself to eat a second portion, and drinking a chocolate shake with two raw eggs. In the beginning, I had to force myself to eat all that. However, in time I desired all that and more.

The second thing I want you to pray for is an opportunity to give your faith away. Ask Him to open the doors of your heart and shutters of your eyes. Ask Him to help you take your eyes off yourself long enough to see the people around you. Get that flow of God moving in your life today. Don't put it off or make excuses. Look for opportunities to encourage, comfort, and teach.

Keep in mind that teaching is not necessarily standing in front of a classroom with a lesson plan, but it is helping other people to walk through life and helping them to discover the goodness of God. Be willing to give away what God has taught you over the years. We can't keep these truths to ourselves; we need that outlet. The greater the intake we have, the greater the outflow we need. The more you receive, the more you can give away. He has created us to have this continual flow in our life. This continual flow brings life to you and those around you.

John 7:37-38: "On the last and greatest day of the Feast, Jesus stood and said in a loud voice, 'If anyone is thirsty, let him come to me and drink. Whoever believes in me, as the scripture has said, streams of living water will flow from within him.'"

Mackenzie is my youngest daughter, 22 years old at the time of this writing. If you know Mackenzie, you know she is the most driven person you will ever want to meet. She started playing soccer when she was just four years old. Yes, we were those soccer parents that drove all over the country and were on the go constantly for several years. She earned a scholarship to play soccer at Truett-McConnell University in Cleveland, Georgia. She played there for two years, and the team won back-to-back Conference Championships for the first time.

But God put something new in her heart, and she left Truett-McConnell, and God opened the door for her to run cross-country at Augusta State University. In her first year of running cross-country at Augusta, she set seven school and course records and became the Peach Belt Cross Country Champion. She won that race by 54 seconds. I say all that to tell you this. There is nobody who will outwork her. I don't care who you are. If you go to the gym with her, you had better be ready to work. Trust me, I know. In the earlier years of her training, I had to limit how much she trained. She is also very particular in what she eats. I really wouldn't call it food because it didn't have any taste. Because of her crazy workout schedule and her choice of lean diet, she began to burn more calories than she was taking in, and over time, she lost a lot of weight and became very unhealthy. Working out is supposed to help you to become healthy, right? How can working out cause someone to not be healthy? It happens when our input can't support our output.

We need that balance in our lives to be spiritually, mentally, and physically healthy. As we grow in wisdom, we require that balance. The stream needs to be constant, and we need to find an outlet to give it away. Find someone to invest in and pour your life into them.

Paul wrote in Second Corinthians 9:6 and said, "Remember this: Whoever sows sparingly will also reap sparingly, and whoever sows generously will also reap generously."

Keep receiving from the Lord and ensure you are full to the point of overflowing, but make sure you cast seeds everywhere you go. It will come back to you many times over.

Chapter 4
Surround Yourself with Godly Influences

Luke 2:52 says, "Jesus grew in wisdom and stature, and in favor with God and man."

Everybody has heard the old saying, "You are what you eat." In other words, what you take into your physical body will determine how healthy or unhealthy you will be down the road. You can't eat Krispy Kreme donuts every day and keep your skinny figure, especially when you get older and your metabolism slows down. Junk in, junk out. There is another phrase I want to introduce to you that may not be as well-known as this first quote: You are who you hang around with. Being in student ministry for nearly thirty years, I have repeated these many times. You may be the nicest, most polite, and well-mannered kid on the face of this earth, but if you hang out with a group of thugs, you will most likely become just like them. The environment you place yourself in as a young believer in Christ will most likely predict your future.

I want to begin this chapter by asking you a couple of questions. I love asking questions that will cause you to think about your life and to see where your life is headed. First question: whom do you spend most of your time with? Second question: what kind of influence are they on you when it comes to living a godly life? Third question: do they make you better, moving you towards a closer relationship with Christ? Fourth question: are they a positive or negative influence on you? I want to encourage you to take the time to think about these questions and think them through. It is

THE TOTAL PACKAGE

a big deal with whom you spend your time. It will affect you as a mom, dad, employee, parent, or even as a mentor.

I was blessed to have the best Youth Pastor in the world. His name was Billy Durham. He was unlike anybody I had ever met. There was something quite special about him. I have had pastors that preached great and could hold my attention, even as a young child. I had godly men in my life but never connected with them as I did with Billy. I knew Billy cared for me. It wasn't just his job he had to do, but he wanted to spend time with me.

One day out of the blue, Billy called me on the house phone. That's right. I said house phone because it was before cell phones. We didn't even have Cable TV. I had three channels to watch. Yes, those were the good ole days when kids went outside and played. My mom answered the phone and said, "Hello." I didn't pay much attention because nobody had ever called our house phone and asked to speak with me. I heard my mom say, "Just a minute, I will get him on the phone." I went to the phone and said, "Hello." It was Billy. Why in the world was a pastor calling me?

Billy simply asked me a question. "Do you want to play basketball?" I must be honest with you, at this point in my life, I didn't know that any kind of pastor had fun. I especially didn't expect them to play ball. Of course, I said, "Sure." He said, "Great, I will come to pick you up in about thirty minutes." Thirty minutes later, he pulled up in a little maroon VW diesel Rabbit, and we took off to play some ball at Pine Glen Subdivision. This subdivision was where all the Eastside guys would come to play basketball and hang out. I found out that day that not only did Billy play ball, but he was good. I have never seen a Christian man want to win so badly.

To say the least, we connected that day. He became one of those people who made me stop and think. He would love me, encourage me, and even get in my face when I needed it. He cared enough about me to attend my football game when I played at Dougherty High. Not only was Billy my friend and Student Pastor, but he also eventually became my brother-in-law. That's right. I married his younger sister. I thank God that I had someone like Billy in my life who taught me about a relationship with God. It was a blessing to have a mentor and friend who taught me how to pray and enjoy reading my Bible. His life was a model for me to follow and pursue. To this day, we still stay connected, and more than ever before, he still encourages me to be all that God has called me to be. Now at 55, I have the privilege of serving with Billy at Park Avenue Baptist Church in Titusville, Florida.

Here are some more questions for you to ponder. Who is your Billy? Who do you have in your life pushing you to grow in wisdom? Who in your life is encouraging you to be more like Christ? You may not have that type of person in your life right now, and I understand because I have been there and done that.

I know how frustrating it is to feel like you are in a spiritual rut and can't move from that spot in life. It's like getting your truck stuck in the mud. This word picture is an excellent South Georgia illustration. So many times in life, we get off the paved road, head down a dirt road, and end up stuck. At first, we try everything to get out. We gather different things around us like limbs, sticks, or anything to shove under our tires to get traction. We get back in the truck and begin by rocking the truck, going forward and backward again and again. Instead of getting out, we are stuck deeper in the mud, and eventually, we say, "What's the use?"

We need each other and those around us who will encourage, motivate, and challenge us to be more like Christ. We all need that person in our life who is willing to meet us where we are at and pull us out of the mud bog of life. If you are in that mud bog of life and don't have that godly mentor, "that Billy," I want to encourage you to do four simple things.

First, start with prayer:

Jeremiah 29:11-13 says, "For I know the plans I have for you," declares the Lord, "plans to prosper you and not to harm you, plans to give you hope and a future. Then you will call upon me and come and pray to me, and I will listen to you. You will seek me and find me when you seek me with all your heart"

Pour out your heart to your heavenly Father. Tell Him exactly what you are feeling and going through. Believe me, He knows precisely what you are facing, but He wants to hear it from you. As a father, I know many things that go on in my kids' lives. Some of those things they didn't have a clue that I already knew. But I wanted to hear it from them. God desires that one-on-one conversation with you. Open yourself up and express your heart to the One who loves you the most. Ask your heavenly Father to open the floodgates of people who can invest in you. Ask God to give you that person that will challenge you to be more like Christ. We all need someone who has walked in our shoes and figured a few things out. It may save you a lot of headaches down the road. You see, God wants you to grow in wisdom. God wants you to become more like Him. Be holy. Why? Because He is holy. He wants to answer your prayers.

Second, keep your spiritual eyes open:

2 Corinthians 4:18 tells us this, "Fix our eyes not on what is seen, but on what is unseen. For what is seen is temporary, but what is unseen is eternal."

What is God trying to show you in the spiritual realm?

Paul prayed over the Church in Ephesus, a prayer that we need to hear today in Ephesians 1:17-18 that says this, "I keep asking that the God of our Lord Jesus Christ, the glorious Father, may give you the Spirit of wisdom and revelation, so that you may know him better. I pray also that the eyes of your heart may be enlightened in order that you may know the hope to which he has called you, the riches of his glorious inheritance in the saints."

Expect God to answer your prayers. How many times in life do we pray and ask God to open a door and close our eyes to the possibilities of what He puts in front of us? Ask Him to help you see people and situations as He would see them. Keep yourself open to His leadership and guidance.

Third, get involved with a local body of believers:

This Christian discipline is a must. Far too many Christians believe Satan's lies that they don't need to go to church.

THE TOTAL PACKAGE

John 10:10 The thief comes only to steal and kill and destroy. I came that they may have life and have it abundantly.

He wants to set you off by yourself where he can pick on you, discourage you, and pick you off without you even realizing it. Get involved with an active small group where you can openly discuss your struggles and weaknesses and compare notes on life. You will discover you are not alone and that other people are struggling with the same issues you are.

Look at what Hebrews 10:25 tell us, "Let us not give up meeting together, as some are in the habit of doing, but let us encourage one another-and all the more as you see the Day approaching."

The author of Hebrews knew that everyone needed that encouragement to live out our Christian faith.

Finally, don't become complacent in your walk with Christ:

Don't settle for the lie that nobody is around you to learn from or mentor you. And don't believe the lie that says you can't teach an old dog new tricks. You must realize that contentment is the number one enemy in becoming a continuous learner or a disciple of Christ.

Proverbs 1:32 says, "For the waywardness of the simple will kill them; and the complacency of fools will destroy you."

Have you ever noticed that when you choose to grow, there always seems to be a struggle? You need resistance to develop. Think about it: to grow stronger physically, you must repeatedly push or pull against something with resistance. In time, you will become stronger. Is it easy? No, it's not. It comes with a cost, and it will take time. Strength and growth will not come overnight. Growing in wisdom is a process involving being open to people God will place around you.

Jesus grew in wisdom. Yes, He was the total package. How are you doing in this first section of this book? We know that God holds all wisdom in His hands and gives it to those who ask. Don't be scared to ask Him for the gift of wisdom. I also challenge you to be that continuous learner and dare to learn new things. Open your life to receive from God what He has for you. Then dare to give it away. Be willing to share with younger believers in Christ, creating a continuous flow of God in your life. Dare to be great. But be sure you surround yourself with godly people who push, encourage, and love you no matter what comes your way. You can do this!

Section 2:
Jesus Grew
In Stature

Chapter 5
Getting to the Starting Line

Luke 2:52 says, "Jesus grew in wisdom and stature, and in favor with God and man."

Jesus grew in stature. In other words, Jesus took care of his physical temple. I must be honest with you; this section of the book has brought my most significant highs and my most immense lows. My physical fitness is like a roller coaster, which is sad but true. I have played ball my whole life. From the day I started walking, I had a ball in my hand, and it all started with a plastic bat and ball. My dad would pitch to me, and I would nail it repeatedly. I never got tired of it. I grew up playing baseball, football, and basketball. As a young boy, I couldn't wait to get outside and play ball with all my neighborhood friends. During the summers, we would play all day long until we had to come in to eat or take a bath for the night. I hated to stop playing to come inside to eat. In those days, food was optional for me.

Oh boy, but how have things now changed in my life? Now at the age of 55, I rarely pick up a ball. Sports have become more of what I watch on TV than something I do. However, I still enjoy exercising and try my best to stay in shape. Most 50-year-olds I know are 30-40 pounds overweight, and they seem to be tied to a chair with a remote in their hands. They have become inactive and have grown to accept it. You may read this book and ask yourself, "How did I get here? I used to be a pretty good athlete." Maybe it was an injury, a medical issue, or just laziness.

THE TOTAL PACKAGE

Now you would be happy if you could just run to the mailbox.

I understand. I have been there. At the age of 43, I was diagnosed with an autoimmune disease. I went from a very conditioned middle-aged athlete to a man who couldn't open a water bottle. No joke! I went from playing two hours of basketball with high school students to being unable to step out of a bathtub. I went to all the doctors and took all kinds of medicines, but I lost my drive to stay healthy. My attitude was terrible, and, to say the least, I was very frustrated. It got so bad that I couldn't physically get out of bed. For the first time in my life, I was not motivated. My fingers and toes would swell and turn purple. My doctors would marvel at how bad it got at such a rapid pace. For four years, I did nothing. I didn't walk, run, jump, or exercise. I took my medicine and felt sorry for myself. To tell you the truth, I had given up and accepted that I would never be the same again.

But thank God, He gave me a wife who didn't give up on me, and she didn't sugar coat it. Laura, my wife, sees everything as black or white. There are no grays in her world. Some people at Laura's work call her "Literal Laura." She doesn't mix words and what you see is what you get. So, she keeps me in check. When everybody felt sorry for me and patted me on the head, Laura would ask, "You're giving up? That is not the man I married!" The gloves came off. She said that without apology, and she didn't stutter. And she didn't stop there. She was on a roll and said, "Get moving! You can't just give up and roll over; you must get off your butt and get active." I will be honest with you. She ticked me off, to say the least. She didn't know what I was facing or how bad I hurt. However, those were the exact words I needed to hear. I made all kinds of excuses, and now I had to find a way to get her off my back. To be honest, I lacked the want to. My passion for exercise was nonexistent. But Laura didn't give up or slow down, and she never let me roll over.

I was humbled during those difficult years. I can still remember the day throwing down a 360 dunk, throwing a baseball 90 plus, and beating down a high school student on the basketball court. Now I couldn't muster up the energy to walk to the neighbor's mailbox without being exhausted. Then Laura spoke the truth to me and said, "You have to start somewhere." In other words, "Get to the starting line."

To me, this was one of the hardest things I've done. But I knew I had to take this first step. I knew I had a long road ahead of me, and it wouldn't be easy. But I had to make a commitment and see this thing through. As I approached the starting line, so many thoughts began to fill my mind, like fears, worries, what ifs, and doubts. I knew there would be setbacks and times when I would ask what I was thinking. Yes, there would be soreness and muscles that would hurt; but I knew it would be worth it, and I was ready for the challenge. I don't know where you are physically, but I want to encourage you to get better and get ready to step onto the line. Make that commitment and stick to it.

Philippians 3:13-14: "Brothers, I do not consider myself yet to have taken hold of it. But one thing I do: Forgetting what is behind and straining toward what is ahead, I press on toward the goal to win the prize for which God has called me heavenward in Christ Jesus."

I am currently the Pastor of Sports and Recreation at Park Avenue Church in Titusville, Florida, and my job is to connect with the community by using sports. One of the first events we organized was a 5K race. I gathered three excellent runners in the church to help me plan this out and pulled in about 70 volunteers to get everything done. I never knew so much work was involved in organizing a race. We had to devise a race route equaling 3.1 miles to make it official, find a crew that would keep up with everyone's time, and develop a good way to have everyone signed into the system. We had to have an approved permit from the city to block the road for a few minutes and a police officer that would stop traffic. We had to buy awards and gather support from local businesses. We also decided to feed everyone pancakes and coffee after the race, so we had to get a whole kitchen crew to cook breakfast for 300 people. Yes, we had race t-shirts and bags with all kinds of free stuff, along with door prizes. I could go on about all the details of putting on a race, but the most difficult challenge was getting people to sign up and commit to running.

    I couldn't tell you how many people said they would run and were so excited, but I never saw their names hit my list. They were just empty words. At one time or another, we all say things that we never follow through and do. How often have we admitted that we are always tired or can't do what we used to do?

    What about your physical condition? On a scale of 1-10, where are you? What are you doing to keep that extra weight off and your heart beating strong? Is your cholesterol level where it needs to be, or is your blood pressure sky high? You must start asking yourself some serious questions. Questions such as, if you continue to stay on the same road you are on physically for the next ten years, what kind of health issues will you face? Will that hinder your quality of life? These statements are a wake-up call for many of you. Don't wait until it's too late. Don't wait until you find out you have heart disease or diabetes. Don't put off what you need to do today. Commit to getting healthy. It is time to get to the starting line. On your mark, get set, and go!

1 Corinthians 6:19-20: "Do you not know that your body is a temple of the Holy Spirit, Who is in you, whom you have received from God? You are not your own; you were bought at a price. Therefore, honor God with your body."

Chapter 6
Little by Little

Luke 2:52 says, "Jesus grew in wisdom and stature, and in favor with God and man."

When we take time to slow down and honestly look at our physical health, it can be very sobering. The truth is, the older we get, the more our health will decline and the more attention we need to give to stay healthy. It's like placing a boiling pot on the back burner and forgetting all about it until it begins to boil over. When we get those warning signs about our decreasing health, we first want to deny it and act as if it is no big deal. We think the issue will disappear if we ignore it and keep living the way we have always lived. But, as time goes on, and we gain more weight and hang on to the bad habits of eating with no exercise, it is evident there is an issue. Instead of denying the fact of being overweight and in bad health, we just dress it up and enjoy it. We find ourselves laughing about not being able to run to the mailbox or making jokes about the size of our plate at a family meal. However, you are dying inside, and you long for the discipline to back away from the table and get outside for a walk. Well, I'm telling you the time is now. No more excuses and no more denying you are out of shape because it is time to do something about it. Talk is cheap.

Proverbs 14:23: "All hard work brings a profit, but mere talk leads only to poverty."

Think of it like this. I am a homeowner responsible for all the maintenance and upkeep of my house and yard. When something breaks around the house, I am responsible for fixing it or getting it fixed. I decide when and who is going to do it. To be honest, there are some things I will put off because I don't want to deal with them, and it will take too much time to fix. So, I ignore the issue and save it for another day, and all the while, the problem worsens. When I ignore the leak in my roof, and I keep putting off repairing it, the more it will cost me to make it right. Do you see where I am going?

Poor physical health is something that deserves our attention. It's not something that we need to put off or act as if it is no big deal. We are responsible for this earthly temple that God has blessed us with. If you are a believer, the Holy Spirit lives inside of you. That means you are a temple and the grounds keeper for His abiding place. He deserves a nice place to live.

Hopefully, if you are still reading, that means you are committed to getting started. The starting line can be scary, but it can also get you pumped up. You have high hopes and adrenaline pumping and are thinking positive thoughts. Now let's move forward and get moving with some practical steps. Whether you set up a home workout area or join the gym, that first workout is so critical and how you go about it. I know I tend to go a little harder than I should because I am motivated and excited about getting back into workout mode. Have you ever been there? That first workout, you go all out. Your energy is high, and you attack the exercise with a ferocious passion. You wrapped up that first workout, and it wasn't as bad as you had imagined, but you went a little harder than you should have. Then the following day, you wake up and feel like a truck has run over you. You are in pain, and even your eyelashes seem to be sore. What were you thinking? Now, all that enthusiasm has left you, motivation has flown out the window, and you are wondering when you will be able to walk again without pain.

I want to give you a few words that helped me immensely: "little by little." You are not going to get back into shape overnight. It has taken you years to develop that belly you have. How many years have you been overeating, sitting on the couch, and doing nothing to improve your health? It will take time to get healthy again. Getting into shape isn't always fun, but it will be worth it.

Hebrews 12:11-12: "No discipline seems pleasant at the time, but painful. Later on, however, it produces a harvest of righteousness and peace for those who have been trained by it. Therefore, strengthen your feeble arms and weak knees."

I want to encourage you before that first workout to take some time to evaluate where you are physically. You must be honest and realistic with yourself. As time passes, your body changes, and so should your workouts. Take time to ask yourself these questions and be honest and practical regarding getting back in shape. How long has it been since I have exercised? What kind of physical limitations do I have? Are there exercises I need to avoid because of that bad shoulder? Do I have any severe health issues? In addition, for some, no joke, you might need to consult with your doctor before starting.

I also want to encourage you to start slowly and ease into a good, steady workout. Little by little, grow into your commitment to become healthy. My physical goals have changed drastically the older I get, and so have my workouts. I no longer try to throw around a lot of heavyweights. There is no grunting or wearing a tank top shirt. My elbow and shoulders hurt too much when I try to bench press 300 pounds. Nowadays, it's about getting that heart rate up.

Exodus 23:29-30 God told Moses, "I will not drive them out in a single year, because the land would become desolate and the wild animals too numerous for you. Little by little I will drive them out before you, until you have increased enough to take possession of the land."

Great things will not happen overnight. It will take hard work, dedication, perseverance, and consistency. Let me tell you about Nehemiah. God called Nehemiah to rebuild the wall around Jerusalem, which was a monumental task. Yes, there would be difficulties to overcome, hoops he had to jump through, and doubts would arise. But Nehemiah stayed focused on the prize. He kept believing in God for the impossible, and he didn't quit when it got hard. In 53 days, he completed the entire wall around Jerusalem. Something that seemed impossible became possible. He kept pushing forward, and he never gave up. He kept thinking, little by little and step-by-step. Getting back into good shape will never be easy, especially the older you are, but it will be worth it. Just remember it is a process, so enjoy the journey. There is an old saying that I love repeating. "How do you eat an elephant? One bite at a time."

Getting back into shape is like remodeling an old house or restoring an old car. It will require a lot of blood, sweat, and tears. You will have to count the cost of what it will take to update the house or restore that car. It will cost you money. You also need a step-by-step plan for how this

THE TOTAL PACKAGE

renovation will take place. That will require a vision to see what it can become when you complete the project. This decision is where you must step in and grind it out. You must follow through with the plans, believe in that vision, and be determined to walk it out. Getting healthy will take time, and it will not happen overnight. Count the cost because it will cost you. Then come up with a plan and make sure you do your research. Then construct a step-by-step plan on how you will reach your end goal. Then put in the work and walk it out. Little by little. Believe me. You have got this.

Philippians 4:13: "I can do everything through him who gives me strength."

Chapter 7
Setting Goals / Accountability

Luke 2:52 says, "Jesus grew in wisdom and stature, and in favor with God and man."

You have approached the starting line. Congratulations! You have started slow, and you are settling into the process. By this time, you should have charted your course. You need a plan, and it needs to be specific and measurable. Think about this. It would be crazy to take a trip to Huntsville, Alabama, without first checking out the best way to get there. Yes, you may know the general direction, but you may waste time and energy getting there. If you are like me, you want the fastest and most direct way to get there. Knowing where you are starting is essential, but knowing your destination is just as important. Then you pick the best route that best suits you and your journey.

I am not looking to be on the cover of a men's muscle magazine, but I would love to lose about ten pounds of belly fat. With that in mind, I will not press a lot of heavy weight and walk around a lot in my workout. I would like to do some light weights with a lot more reps. Maybe use the stationary bike to warm up and then get in a couple of miles on an elliptical trainer. Come up with a plan and set your goals. I strongly encourage you to write your plan down as you head in a specific direction. Then walk it out. I want to encourage you to be realistic and keep thinking little by little. You see, goal setting involves developing an action plan to motivate and guide a person towards a goal.

THE TOTAL PACKAGE

Here are some important questions you must ask yourself when setting your goals. What will be the best time for me to work out? There is no doubt that we are all busy and we have so many things going on. We have our work schedule, family events, church, and many other things that pile up. Start by blocking out a thirty-minute session of time each day to work out. Get into a routine and try your best to be consistent. As time passes, look to slowly increase your time as you work into the groove of exercising. Consistency is a huge key to becoming fit.

James 1:4: "Perseverance must finish its work so that you may be mature and complete, not lacking anything."

The second question you need to ask yourself is what workout will best help you achieve your goals. Over the years, my activity has changed drastically. In my younger days, I would go to the weight room to lift heavy weights. My goal was to gain more muscle mass and get stronger. Growing up, I was that skinny kid who looked like he needed worming. I could eat all I wanted, but I could never gain any weight or muscle. I remember stuffing myself with food and down a protein milkshake with eggs. I would try my best to get in five meals daily yet never gain a pound. However, times have changed. Now at 55, I have stepped away from the weights and have upped my cardio. I also must watch what I eat. I am no longer the all-you-can-eat food bars guy. Our bodies change, and so should our workouts and diet.

I want to encourage you to talk to other people who are knowledgeable about working out. For example, if I wanted to put on muscle mass, I wouldn't listen to the advice of someone who is a 135 lb. wormy guy. Or, if I wanted to up my cardio game, I sure wouldn't take the advice of someone who weighed over 300 pounds and could barely walk across the street. Listen to the person who not only has the head knowledge but one who walks it out daily. Do your research. Take time to Google and read about all the different types of exercise. Don't be scared to try a couple of routines before focusing on one workout. Also, make your workout as fun as possible and keep your eyes on the end goal.

After you write out your goals, ensure they stay in front of you. Post them in places you go every day. Tape them to the mirror in your bathroom or your car's dash. Place a note and run them through your mind as you wash dishes or cook. It will be a constant reminder of your commitment to getting healthy. Let's be honest with each other. We all need motivation along the way. Use every tool possible to stay the course. I am at that stage of life where I am not worried about how much I can bench press or how far I can hit a softball. But I want to be healthy enough to walk my daughters down the aisle when they marry. I want to be able to get down on the floor to play with my future grandkids. Set those goals, spell them out, and go for it.

Habakkuk 2:2-3: "Write down the revelation and make it plain on tablets so that a herald may run with it. For the revelation awaits an appointed time; it speaks of the end and will not prove false. Though it lingers, wait for it; it will certainly come and will not delay."

You have reached the starting line and are committed to getting healthy. You have set some goals and even wrote them down as a reminder. You kick off the workout routine and have a couple of workouts under your belt. But your body is sore, you are much more tired than usual, and you

THE TOTAL PACKAGE

begin to wonder if all this is worth it. That drive and passion you once had have left the building. Plus, things at work have picked up, and the kids have just kicked up for another soccer season. Have you ever been there?

    I don't know about you, but I can come up with so many excuses to skip a workout. I can't tell you how many times I have taken my gym bag to work with the idea of going by the gym and getting in a quick workout before I cut the grass at home. But something clicked in my mind. I could have the grass done by 6:00 PM, have supper on the table by 6:30, and chill out the rest of the night in my recliner. Then I ride past the gym. At first, I would feel bad about the decision I had just made to skip the gym, but then I reasoned in my head that cutting grass could be my workout for the day. Yeah, that's it. Now I have an excuse, and I don't have to feel bad about it. Have you ever noticed that skipping one workout makes it much easier to cut the next one too?

    Here is where we need accountability. For us to be our best and achieve our goals, we all need someone in our lives that will encourage us to stay the course and push us and even get in our face if required. Do you have that kind of person in your life? If I can be honest with you for a moment, if I had to graft my physical health on a chart, it would be all over the place. It is sad to say, but that is the truth. There would be some high points where I was in pretty good shape for a 50-year-old man, but there would be some serious valleys too. Most of us can relate to that. I have that kind of personality where I am all in, or I am over it. I am super motivated, or I am looking for the next challenge. That has been a major struggle for me for my entire life. I need balance and consistency. That is why God has placed Luke 2:52 in my heart, and that is why I am trying my best to write this book. I know the struggle of losing focus and pushing my goals to the side. I know what it's like to quit things when times get hard or things are not quite what I thought they would be.

Accountability is necessary if we want to achieve our goals and dreams. Accountability to me is a partnership between two people that says, "I will be there for you, and I will encourage you to be your best." When I am tempted to pass by the gym to go and cut grass at the house, my partner will call me on my cell and say, "Where are you? I am waiting for you?" So, I will then turn around and head back to the gym. At that moment, I am ticked off. I don't feel like working out today, but I just got called out. I show up, and I get the workout in, and of course, I am glad I did. As I leave, I slap my buddy's hand and tell him thanks.

I don't care what level you are at physically. Whether we are professional athletes or a 50-year-old want-to-be, we all need accountability and encouragement to achieve our goals. Professional athletes pay trainers to improve and push them beyond what they think they could do. Those trainers find ways to motivate their clients to be their very best. For us, that accountability partner can be your best friend, spouse, and even your daughter. Know this. God will give you everything you need to be successful and the people you need to get healthy. Take time to look around and see whom He has placed around you.

For me to be healthy, not only do I need regular exercise, but I also need a continuous flow of water. I will admit I love drinking coffee and cokes. I know it is not the preferred health drink, but that is what my body craves. Over the years, I have struggled with kidney stones. Let me tell you, having kidney stones is very painful. It will put a powerful man on his knees and cause him to curl up into a fetal position. I don't care who you are or how tough you claim to be. After three kidney stones, I finally decided to listen to my doctor, stop drinking so many dark liquids, and start drinking more water or clear fluids. My wife Laura heard that advice from my doctor, who has appointed herself as my accountability partner. Notice I said, "She appointed herself as my accountability partner." She wasn't my first choice.

Drinking water sounds like an easy thing to do to avoid so much pain, but I am very hardheaded and a very slow learner. Water has no taste, and I hated drinking something with no flavor. I always did well right after passing that kidney stone, but as time passed, I forgot all about the pain. Then I slow down on my water intake again, and I again experience the pain of another kidney stone.

I will say this. Laura is your person if you need an accountability partner to hold you accountable for something. She doesn't mind hurting your feelings or ticking you off. If you want accountability, you will get it whether you like it or not. I cannot tell you how many days straight she has asked me, "How many waters have you had today?" Not a day goes by when she doesn't ask me that question. Of course, it is never enough. Then she comes with a bottle of water in her hand and says, "Drink it." Do you know how old that question gets to me? You think she would get tired of asking that same question repeatedly, but she knows me and knows I need to drink water to be healthy and avoid pain. She cares enough to ask every single day. Do you have that "Laura" in your life? We all need that type of person in our life to get better and achieve our goals in life. Who is in your corner? Who is that person who will call you out? Ask God to give you people around you who care enough to hold you to a higher standard.

Chapter 8
Not a Diet

Luke 2:52 says, "Jesus grew in wisdom and stature, and in favor with God and man."

To me, a diet is something you do for a short period, and it's a temporary change from the food we eat on a routine basis. I have known some people who have lost a lot of weight by going on a diet, and I have seen so many moms get pumped up right before their daughter's wedding and lose incredible amounts of weight to fit into a specific size dress. Then when the wedding is over, they return to their old way of living and eating. There are more diets today than ever before, but there seem to be more overweight people than I can ever remember. You see, we don't need a diet plan, but we need a lifestyle change. I hate to oversimplify things, but I think we make losing weight too complicated. Being healthy is about making good choices, eating smart, and exercising daily. And when you bring God into your healthy eating, it changes everything. Striving to honor Him in your food and drink choices will bring not only a heart change but it will change your choices.

1 Corinthians 10:31: "So whether you eat or drink or whatever you do, do it all for the glory of God."

For many of us, our metabolism has slowed down quite a bit, but we continue to eat the way we did when we were in our 20s. I do believe we need to avoid certain things in our diets, especially the older we are. I have tried to avoid fried food in the last couple of years. I know what you are thinking. Dennis, you have gone too far now. I just lost half my readers. I will be honest with you; there is nothing better than some deep-fried chicken cooked up in some Crisco grease. Can I get an Amen? But it is not a healthy option. Now, there will be times when I push everything to the side, and I will eat that piece of fried chicken because it tastes so good. However, I am not eating it every week.

I also avoid high sugar drinks, like sodas and good South Georgia sweet tea. I grew up on sweet tea, which was always in our refrigerator. I remember drinking gallon after gallon of my mama's sweet tea. Now, if you wanted some good, sweet tea, you needed to go to my grandmother's house and get some of that tea. It was so good.

Proverbs 25:27: "It is not good to eat too much honey. Nor is it honorable to seek one's own honor."

The third thing we need to cut back on is our bread intake. I know what you are thinking; can we eat anything good? Notice I said, "We need to cut back on our bread intake." We still must live and enjoy life, right? I love bread, especially the bread at Outback Steakhouse. Back in the day, I could eat five loaves covered in butter all by myself. My metabolism has changed, and those days are only a memory now.

I said all that to say this. I want to encourage you not to get lost in some diet that lasts for a short period. Yes, you may lose a couple extra pounds, but in most cases, that weight returns and brings a couple more pounds. Watch those fried foods, sugar intake, and those additional amounts of bread. But here is the difference maker, are you ready for this? The rubber meets the road here, especially for a guy: it's the one-plate rule. You heard me right. We must maintain the one plate rule and no stacking. The one plate rule is where you only have one plate of food at each meal, and there are no seconds. If you want a dessert, it must be on that one plate, not a separate plate. I believe you can still enjoy good food, but you need to watch your portions. I can remember many meals when I had two plates of food, and they were stacked to the hilt, and then I went back for a plate of desserts. Notice that the dessert had an "s " on it. No stacking means you must stop loading up your plate, and you can't let your portions touch each other. Don't pile a portion of mashed potatoes on top of your pile of peas just to make room on your one plate.

I am not a dietician or some health guru. I am just a guy who has been there and done that. I believe you can be healthy and enjoy all kinds of food. You don't need a diet, but you do need a lifestyle change. You will not see fast weight loss results like some diets, but it will be a gradual and steady weight loss and a road to a healthier you. It's not a program you do for two months and then go back to how you were living. It will take discipline and a commitment to see this through, but I guarantee you will thank yourself ten years later. You can still enjoy good food and get healthier as you live life. Not many of us will be Olympians or be on the cover of a muscle magazine, but we want to live long enough to see our kids get married and play with our grandchildren on the floor. I don't know about you, but I want to be able to run and play hide and seek until I'm 70 years old.

What are you putting into your bodies? What kind of fuel are you receiving? We all have different body types; some of us are built like a racecar, where we are leaner and faster. You are on the move, and you are still full of energy.

THE TOTAL PACKAGE

Others are built like a pickup truck; everything still works, and all your windows are rolled up, and you are still active and useful, but you don't have the energy you once had.

I drive a 2005 Chevrolet Colorado pickup truck with over 200,000 miles. I never take it on long trips, but I drive it every day from point A to point B. It's not in the prime of life, and it does have its limitations. None of the windows roll down, and my air conditioner only works when it is set on high. Because of the age of my truck, when heavy rains come, it does tend to leak quite a bit. But she keeps cranking up and has not let me down when I need to go somewhere. From a racecar to the old Chevrolet Colorado truck, all need good fuel to keep running. Yes, and they will all need a good oil change along the way. Don't expect a racecar to perform at a high level with bad fuel. Decide today to make that lifestyle change and find a good consistent workout that becomes a critical part of your life. Steady, but sure.

1 Corinthians 6:12: "Everything is permissible for me"-but not everything is beneficial. 'Everything is permissible for me-but I will not be mastered by anything."

Don't allow food to master you. In closing out this session, I want to encourage you to get to the starting line to have a better you. Take time to evaluate your physical condition and devise a plan that works best for you. Start slow but be consistent. Spell out your goals and make them measurable. Find that person or group who will encourage you along the way or get in your face when you need it the most. Commit to watching what you eat and how much you eat. You don't need a diet, but you must make healthy lifestyle changes to benefit your future health. And along the way, don't forget to celebrate the victories and enjoy the process. Don't get so caught up in the grind that you forget to enjoy life. This closes out the second step to becoming that total package, just like Jesus. Make sure you take care of the temple God has given you.

Section 3:
Jesus Grew
In Favor With God

Chapter 9
Break Down the Walls

Luke 2:52 And Jesus increased in wisdom and in stature and in favor with God and man.

Jesus grew in favor with God. He grew in His relationship with His Father. How often have we read where Jesus got alone with His Father to pray? After long days of ministry and loving on people, He knew it was a must to go and be refreshed.

Matthew 14:22-23 says this, "Immediately Jesus made the disciples get into the boat and go on ahead of him to the other side, while he dismissed the crowd. After he dismissed them, he went up on a mountainside by himself to pray."

If Jesus had to spend time with the Father, how much more do we need to do the same? We will have obstacles, hard times, and overwhelming situations in this life. There will be times when we fail God and maybe even disappoint ourselves. Think about it, many of the all-time greats in God's Word messed up big time. They fell short, and they didn't make the grade. Yes, they sinned and even doubted Jesus. Look at the life of David. David was called a man after God's own heart. What a compliment! That would be a great name to put on the back of a T-shirt. Growing up as a child in middle school, nicknames were huge. All my friends had a nickname or two. We hit that phase in life where we thought calling each friend by their mom's name was hilarious. I cannot tell you how much fun we had doing that.

THE TOTAL PACKAGE

I know that sounds crazy, but that was typical middle school stuff.

I remember as a middle schooler wanting to change my hairstyle. Up to this point in life, I didn't care what my hair looked like. I only took a shower because my mom told me to. Deodorant was an option. One day I decided to go with what I called the butt-cut. That was the hairstyle with the part right down the middle of your head, and then you would wing it back on both sides. And here was the secret to the new look: spray it down with hairspray while it was still wet. Don't get jealous. I was looking good. This unique hairstyle gave me a huge confidence boost. So, I decided to reveal the new Dennis at our church's men's softball game. I took time to fix my hair just right, and then the whole family got in the car and headed to the game. We were running a little late. The game had already started, and the people from the church were already in the stands. As I walked up, everybody took notice of my new hairstyle. I had the butt cut looking good, and it was slicked back. Then one of the college guys in the stand stood up and yelled out, "Slick." I was never so proud; I had a new nickname. I was so proud of that new nickname that I put it on the back of a t-shirt, and I wore that shirt proudly.

David might not have put his nickname on the back of a shirt, but it was the greatest nickname of all times. However, even with the greatest nickname ever, David still messed up. David fell short. His spiritual wall collapsed. He made some terrible decisions, which started with lusting over Bathsheba. He could have walked away, but lust grabbed his heart and took him to a place he never wanted to go. That lust led him to adultery, murder, and big-time regret. Because of this sin, David's relationship with God was damaged, and a wall was placed between David and God.

Psalm 51:1-4 David tells us this. "Have mercy on me, O God, according to your unfailing love; according to your great compassion blot out my transgressions. Wash away all my iniquity and cleanse me from my sin. For I know my transgressions, and my sin is always before me. Against you, you only, have I sinned and done what is evil in your sight, so that you are proved right when you speak and justified when you judge."

I want you to take this time to look closely at your own life. It is always good when we take time to reflect on our hurts, disappointments, fears, and our sins. It is easy to avoid these topics and keep living life like they do not exist, but it is necessary. When was the last time you sat down with God and poured your heart out to Him? I encourage you to drop the pretense with God that everything is good. He knows exactly what you are struggling with, your thought life, motives, anger issues, depression, jealousy, and life regrets. David tried his best to cover up his sin, but he kept getting deeper into the lies. I encourage you to read 2 Samuel 11 and see how David attempted to cover up his adultery with lies and deceit. David thought everything was covered up and under control, but things worsened. His adultery led to murder. Have you ever noticed sin has a way of getting out in the open? Sin will find you out, take you places you never intended to go and keep you longer than you wanted to stay. Not only does our sin affect us, but it also affects the people around us.

Eventually, David's sin caught up with him. He thought he had pushed it all under the rug and covered it perfectly. Nobody would ever know, but God was about to bring his sin out in the open.

2 Samuel 12:1-7; tells us this, "The Lord sent Nathan to David. When he came to him, he said, 'There were two men in a certain town, one rich and the other poor. The rich man had a very large number of sheep and cattle, but the poor man had nothing except one little ewe lamb he had bought. He raised it and grew up with him and his children. It shared his food, drank from his cup, and slept in his arms. It was like a daughter to him. Now a traveler came to the rich man, but the rich man refrained from taking one of his sheep or cattle to prepare a meal for the traveler who had come to him.' Instead, he took the ewe lamb that belonged to the poor man and prepared it for the one who had come to him. David burned in anger against the man and said to Nathan, 'As surely as the Lord lives, the man who did this deserves to die! He must pay for that lamb four times over, because he did such a thing and had no pity.' Then Nathan said to David, 'You are the man!'"

David's sin was exposed! His sin found him out. Look at David's response in verse 13. David said, "I have sinned against God."

The reality of his sin slapped him in the face, and he was overwhelmed with guilt and shame. He realized God saw it all. How did David, a man after God's own heart, get here? How did he fall so far? Over time, he built a wall of pride and selfishness, and his heart was full of lust and selfish desires. This wall of sin had affected his relationship with his Heavenly Father. Look what happened in Psalm 51. David realized what he did was wrong, and he had to be honest with himself and the Lord.

Psalm 51:7-12 says, "Clean me with hyssop, and I will be clean; wash me, and I will be whiter than snow. Let me hear joy and gladness; let the bones you have crushed rejoice. Hide your face from my sins and blot out all my iniquity. Create in me a pure heart, O God, and renew a steadfast spirit within me. Do not cast me from your presence or take your Holy Spirit from me. Restore to me the joy of your salvation and grant me a willing spirit, to sustain me."

David saw his sins, and he turned to the Lord and repented. He cried out to God and asked Him to forgive him, wipe his sin away, and give him a clean heart.

This heart of repentance is where transformation begins. We need to return to our first love. Ask yourself some serious questions. Where is the passion I once had for Jesus? Where is that desire I used to have for God's Word? What happened to the compassion I once had for other people? When did I start pushing God away and start living for my purposes? It's time to have a Psalm 51 conversation with God. It is time to come clean and be open and honest with God.

1 John 1:9 says, "If we confess our sins, he is faithful and just and will forgive us our sins and purify us from all unrighteousness."

Stop right where you are and ask God for forgiveness. Confess your sin fully with God and hold nothing back. It is time to dump that heavy load of guilt and sin you have been carrying for years. It is time to lay it at the feet of Jesus. What walls need to come down in your life? Is it that secret sin that has haunted you for years and years? Is it a lustful heart? How about that pride and selfishness? Whatever it is, it can fall if we would just bring it to the Lord. Lay it at his feet and trust him with it. Then leave it there.

Chapter 10
Build a Strong Foundation

Luke 2:52 And Jesus increased in wisdom and in stature and in favor with God and man.

We all have those times when we must tear down the walls we have allowed to exist. We all fall short, and we all mess up, and we do mess up along the way. But it is so good to have a God who understands and shows us so much grace. "Thank you, Lord, for the gift of forgiveness and mercy. Thank you for lifting me and encouraging me daily. Thank you, God, for the privilege to come before you when I need to say, 'I am sorry.' Thank you for tearing down that old wall of sin in my heart." Yes, be thankful, but this is just the beginning of what God has for us as children of God. Not only does God want to break down the old walls of our lives, but He also wants us to build a firm foundation that will stand strong even when the worst storms come our way.

Matthew 7: 24-25 Jesus tells us this, "Therefore everyone who hears these words of mine and puts them into practice is like a wise man who built his house on the rock. The rain came down, the streams rose, and the winds blew and beat against that house; yet it did not fall, because it had its foundation on the rock."

What is your life built on? Before I go any further, my heart desires to make sure you have a personal walk with Jesus Christ. Has there been a time in your life when you

THE TOTAL PACKAGE

have come face-to-face with Jesus? Have you had an encounter with the Living God of the universe? Being a Christian, a follower of Christ isn't about our church attendance. It is not about doing good deeds or being morally good. It is about having a personal relationship with Jesus and making Him the foundation on which everything is built. Being a Christian is knowing that the eternal God made a way for us to come to Him. Knowing and believing that He gave us His one and only Son to die on an old rugged cross, but also believing Jesus didn't stay in that grave. This foundation is knowing that Jesus overcame sin and death, and He is alive and well today. "Thank you, Lord!"

Revelations 3:20 says this, "Here I am. Behold I stand at the door and knock. If anyone hears my voice and opens the door, I will come in and eat with him, and he with me."

Have you answered that knock? Have you given your life to Jesus? Have you told Him, "Thank you" for what He has done for you? Have you ever asked him to come in and take over? Here is where it all begins.

Every builder needs to have a solid foundation. It needs to meet certain specifications. It must be able to handle the weight of the load. That foundation in a believer's life is a personal relationship with Jesus Christ. When the storms come, and the water rises, will your foundation be able to stand? Money, power, position, and popularity will crumble under the weight of the load. Build on something that will last, something that will stand the test of time. When we come to the end of ourselves and receive Jesus as our Lord and Savior, He becomes that foundation forever and ever. Yes, there will be tough times in life, and there will be struggles along the way.

Hebrews 13:5 reads like this, "Keep your lives free from the love of money and be content with what you have, because God has said, "Never will I leave you; never will I forsake you."

That is a promise from God Himself. He is my protector and my Heavenly Father. The great I AM. The God of heaven and earth. The all-knowing and all-powerful God of the universe, and I call Him Father, because of what Jesus has done for me.

Oprah Winfrey has gone on record to say, "There are many ways to God." I want to go on record to say, "That is a lie from the very pit of Hell."

Jesus tells us in John 14:6, "I am the way, the truth, and the life. No one comes to the Father except through me."

In other words, Jesus said there is only one way to have a life-changing relationship with God. You can't be good enough to earn salvation or get a golden ticket to heaven. You can go to church every single time the church door opens and still spend eternity in Hell forever and ever. You can study your Bible from cover to cover and memorize hundreds of verses and still fall short of the kingdom of God. You can be dunked in the baptismal pool at your church five times and still be lost in Satan's web of lies. We serve a Holy God that can have nothing to do with sin. Sin separated us from God, and a price had to be paid for our sins. God had a plan, and He sent His only Son in the form of a baby to be born of a virgin. This baby would live the perfect life without sin and become God's perfect Lamb. He willingly laid down His life on that old rugged cross for us.

THE TOTAL PACKAGE

2 Corinthians 5:21 says, "God made him "Jesus" who had no sin to be sin for us, so that in him we might become the righteousness of God."

Jesus suffered, bled, and died for us. In other words, he took my place! He took my punishment and suffering. And the good news is this: death could not hold Him; the grave could not keep him. Three days later, he arose from the grave, and he is alive and well today, and he sits at the right hand of the Father. But the most essential point is this. He rules upon the throne of my heart, and He has changed my life forever. "Thank you, Lord." That is the good news of Jesus in a nutshell.

Have you received that Truth in your life? Are you building your life on the foundation of Jesus? When the winds blow, and the storms come in life, will your life hold up under all the pressures? Receive the Good News today and allow Him to take over.

Chapter 11
Build on It

Luke 2:52 And Jesus increased in wisdom and in stature and in favor with God and man.

I don't want to oversimplify our relationship with God, but I believe we try to make things too complicated. God is calling us today to tear down the walls that hinder our relationship with a Holy God and open our eyes to see the things that separate us from sweet fellowship with the Father. There must be a time of reflection and confession. We must dump that burden of sin and guilt and experience the freedom found in the grace and mercy of Jesus. Then lay that foundation that will stand the test of time. That foundation is found only in Jesus Christ.

My sister and brother-in-law built a beautiful two-story house on three acres of land about 15 years ago. It is a lovely home, but after so many years, they wanted to do a few updates to give it a new look. So, they decided to rip up the old carpet, tile, and another flooring to put down hardwood floors downstairs. They contracted with a company to get all this work done, and the contractors started on the job and began to rip out and bust up all the old flooring. After all the old flooring was gone, the contractors started to place the new hardwood on the concrete foundation. As they began to install the new wood, in just a few minutes of work, they noticed the new wood was popping up for some reason. It wouldn't stay down. To make a long story short, the foundation was not properly leveled out when the foundation was poured, and that was causing the hardwood floors not to lay down properly. To say the least, this was not good news for my sister. To correct the problem, another company was called in to make the foundation level before they could lay the new hardwood. The cost of the installation just doubled. Everything hinged on the foundation. That is why it is so essential to build your foundation on Jesus. Everything starts and ends with the foundation.

Jesus spoke in Matthew 7:24-27 and said, "Therefore everyone who hears these words of mine and puts them into practice is like a wise man who built his house on the rock. The rain came down, the streams rose, and the winds blew and beat against that house, yet it did not fall, because it had its foundation on the rock. But everyone who hears these words of mine and does not put them into practice is like a foolish man who built his house on sand. Then the rains came down, the streams rose, and the winds blew and beat against that house, and it fell with a great crash."

Now it is time to build on that foundation of Jesus. This foundation is the beginning of a lifelong journey and a process of growth. So many Christians come to this place in their life, where they receive Jesus as Savior. They have their golden ticket, they are safe from the fires of Hell, and their relationship doesn't go any further. God wants to open the door to a whole new world, and He is calling everyone to build on this newly discovered relationship.

I have built two houses in my lifetime, and I promised myself I would never do that again. The second house we built was a lot smoother than the first, but neither house was an easy task. It took time, patience, and a lot of money. How crazy would it be if I chose a contractor and began to prepare the ground for the foundation? Then they would set the forms, pour all that concrete, and smooth it out where it would dry and harden. Getting the foundation ready is a huge deal.

What would you say to me if I just walked away and never finished building my house? You would think I was crazy, right? Why would I go to all that trouble and effort and then walk away? There would be so much more to do and experience. Coming to the end of a building experience is exciting and satisfying. To see the result is so gratifying. Not everything went perfectly, and there were mess-ups along the way, but I kept plugging and didn't give up. You know there were things I wished I had done differently or things I wished I had spent the extra money to do, like adding an outside doorway from the garage. That way, I wouldn't have to open my overhead door whenever I walk out of my garage.

It's crazy to say, but I started my spiritual foundation when I was five years old. I received Jesus at Pine Bluff Baptist Church in Albany, Georgia. I remember it like it was yesterday. Did I understand everything about God? No. But I knew I was lost and empty without Him in my life. I heard the call of Christ, and I answered that call. For years, my foundation sat there empty, and I never knew there was more to being a child of God. I was that church kid who never missed a service. My family went every time the doors were open. My family even mowed the churchyard, and that also included the graveyard. Our church then had a bus ministry, and my dad was one of the drivers. I have many memories of getting on that bus and going around the community to pick up little kids. I was doing church with the best of them. I was living the perfect Christian life, so I thought.

THE TOTAL PACKAGE

Years down the road, we went to another church in the community. There I met the Youth Pastor, whose name was Billy Durham. You will hear more about him as the book continues. This guy opened the door to my spirit that has changed my life forever. Billy took us to a youth retreat in Norman Park, Georgia. I didn't want to go, but all my friends were going to be there, and I knew this place had a gym. So, I decided to go because I thought I would have a fun time, but I had no clue that God had just set me up. That weekend we were introduced to the concept of spending time alone with God. Billy gave us all a spiritual journal. I will be honest with you. My first thought was, this is girly because only girls journal. I am so serious when I say that, but Billy proceeded to share how his time alone with God had changed his life. This concept of a time alone with God blew me away as a 10th grader in high school. That weekend changed my life forever, and I will never be the same.

If you want to build on the foundation of Jesus Christ, you must start with a time alone with God. Some call this their quiet time. As believers in Christ, we need time to soak in the presence of God. I love to say it like this, grilled chicken is good, but when you marinate it in sauce, chicken just goes to the next level. When we make that commitment to soak or marinate in the very presence of God, He will take us to another level of living. But it starts with a commitment.

First, set aside time every day to meet with the Lord. Block that time out every day. This dedicated time is where you make your relationship with God a priority.

Psalm 143:8: "Let the morning bring me word of unfailing love, for I have put my trust in you. Show me the way I should go, for you I lift up my soul."

I strongly advocate meeting with God first thing in the morning. I want to get my marching orders and the directions I will need for the day. There are days when I will need all the wisdom and encouragement I can get. Jesus himself took time in the morning to spend with his Father.

Mark 1:35: "Very early in the morning, while it was still dark, Jesus got up, left the house and went off to a solitary place, where he prayed."

Don't forget that Jesus is our greatest example. Yes, He is the total package. If our Lord Jesus Christ needed his time alone with God, how much more do we need this time? Just know this, if the devil can't make you bad, he will make you busy.

Imagine you were on a trip, you have been driving for some time, but you are on a tight time schedule and in a rush to get to your destination. You are running out of gas, and you need to stop to refuel. You finally find a gas station, but you have so much happened in your life, and you are running a little late. A man is attending the pumps, waiting for you to stop to fill up your gas tank in your car, but you are in such a hurry you don't have time to stop. You keep riding around the gas pump, telling the attendant to give you 20 dollars' worth. In the gas attendant's frustration, he does his best job hitting your gas tank. However, most of the gas ended up on the ground. Then you pull away, and you take off on your journey. I know that sounds crazy and probably will never happen in real life, but that is what is happening in many of your lives. You stay so busy, running from one appointment to another, never slowing down, and you are running on empty. Sooner or later, you will be left beside the road physically, mentally, and emotionally empty.

THE TOTAL PACKAGE

We all need to hear this simple truth, slow down. Learn how to enjoy your time alone with God. Take time to soak in His presence and receive from your Heavenly Father. Get away from all the distractions of life. Get away from the cell phone, emails, and all the electronics. Find a quiet place and commit to meeting with Him every day. You may be asking, why are you stressing the importance of meeting with God? Why is this time so important? Because it is important to Him, and He created us for fellowship. Ok, Dennis. I will block out time for God. Now what?

Now, spend time in prayer. Prayer is a conversation with God that involves talking with Him. As a father, nothing is more enjoyable than sitting down and listening to my girls talk about their lives. That includes the good times and the tough times. When we all get together during a school break or for the holidays, we will go to the nearest coffee shop and just talk for hours.

Jeremiah 33:3: "Call to me and I will answer you and tell you great and unsearchable things you do not know."

Most of us have the talking part down. God loves to hear you talk and come to Him with your problems in life. But a conversation is both talking and listening. Don't just lay your heart out to God and then take off. Take time to listen to what He has to say back to you. I beg you to read one of my favorite books ever, *"Hearing God"* by Peter Lord. To me, this is the best book to help you understand how important it is to take time to listen to God. I had the privilege to sit in Pastor Lord's home and learn from someone who has heard from God. When Christians pray, most realize that they are speaking to God, but many don't understand that God speaks back to them. They never take time to listen for His response.

John 10:27: "My sheep listen to my voice; I know them, and they follow me."

John 16:13: "But when he, the Spirit of truth, comes, he will guide you in all truth. He will not speak on his own; he will speak only what he hears, and he will tell you what is yet to come."

Hearing God is vital to that intimate relationship that He desires from us. The word "vital" is something perceived as necessary to live. The greatest tragedy in a Christian's life is that most of us only turn to God when we are in a crisis. Well, if the only time you come to God is in an emergency, guess what God will send your way?

Luke 10:38-40: "As Jesus and his disciples were on their way, he came to a village where a woman named Martha opened her home to him. She had a sister called Mary, who sat at the Lord's feet listening to what he said. But Martha was distracted by all the preparations that had to be made. She came to him and asked, 'Lord, don't you care that my sister has left me to do the work by myself. Tell her to help me!'"

Look at Jesus' response in Luke 10:41-42, "Martha, Martha," the Lord answered, 'you are worried and upset about many things, but only one thing is needed. Mary has chosen what is better, and it will not be taken from her.'"

What does Jesus desire the most from us? It's not our work or what we can accomplish. He wants us to take time to sit at his feet and soak in His presence. He desires our fellowship more than anything. King David had many struggles in life and faced some hardship, but he held on and never gave up because God was his high tower, shelter, and stronghold. Look what David says in Psalm 27:1-5:

"The Lord is my light and my salvation-whom shall, I fear? The Lord is my stronghold of my life-of whom shall I be afraid? When evil men advance against me to devour my flesh, when my enemies and my foes attack me, they will stumble and fall. Though an army besiege me, my heart will not fear; though war breaks out against me, even then will I be confident."

How could David be so confident, strong, unwavering, and sure?

Psalm 27:4; David said, "One thing I ask of the Lord, this is what I seek; that I may dwell in the house of the Lord all the days of my life, to gaze upon the beauty of the Lord and to seek him in his temple."

David chose to seek, gaze, and dwell in the Lord. He chose to sit at God's feet and soak in His presence. David decided to gaze at his heavenly Father and glance at everything else. He dwelt with God, which means this became a lifestyle, a way of life for David. David discovered how he could have an intimate relationship with God. He chose the best thing in life, the one thing that mattered. Just like Mary in Luke 10, David made it a priority to sit at the feet of the Father. He chose to soak in God's presence.

1 Thessalonians 5:17-18: "Pray continually; give thanks in all circumstances, for this is God's will for you in Christ Jesus."

Pray continually means to talk and listen to the Father throughout your day and be thankful for all the blessings of life. God is good, and He is good all the time! Prayer can change your world, and it can even change your attitude about life. If you are a worrier, start praying. If you are depressed and overwhelmed, pray. You see, worrying is taking responsibility for something God never attended for us to handle. In whom or what do we put our trust? I want to give you three things that will help you to stay focused on the main thing.

1. Make deliberate choices and efforts to set your mind on Christ.

Colossians 3:1, "Since then, you have been raised with Christ, set your hearts on things above, where Christ is seated at the right hand of God."

2. Make a deliberate choice to exercise your mind on Christ. In other words, practice His presence. Keep a continuous conversation going with your Heavenly Father.

3. Carry this exercise of setting your mind on God in every area of life. It doesn't matter how small or how big the situation is.

I also want to encourage you to pray specifically. You will see the very power of God. I also want you to take another step forward and encourage you to write in a journal. Begin to write down your prayers and what God is showing you. Your prayer life will come alive. God is calling His Church to pray and to pray with actions.

Chapter 12
Open God's Love Letter

Luke 2:52 And Jesus increased in wisdom and in stature and in favor with God and man.

Joshua 1:8 tells us this, "Do not let the Book of the Law depart from your mouth; meditate on it day and night, so that you may be careful to do everything written in it."

We need God's Word in our life. We need a steady diet of Truth in our spiritual diet. It is time for men and women of God to meditate on the Holy Scriptures and to hide all its truth in our hearts. If we are going to follow Jesus, reading God's Word is a must.

During my time in college, I had to travel about two hours from home to get there. For me, this was tuff. I have always been a mama's boy and am very proud of it. Honestly, my mom did everything for me. She spoiled me with all her love. But the love of my life was also two hours away. Yes, I am talking about Laura Durham, my future bride-to-be! Now keep in mind there were no cell phones and no FaceTime. There was only a pay phone downstairs in the dorm buildings, and there was no such thing as emails or texts. It is incredible how far we have come with technology. I am not sure if it is a good thing or not. How would kids today survive in the '80s? Our only form of communication was by writing letters.

I remember walking to the Student Center every day, hoping to see a letter from my beautiful girlfriend. There were days when I opened my mailbox, and there were no letters. The disappointment was overwhelming. I do remember those days when I opened my mailbox and I would see a letter from my future wife. I couldn't contain my joy and excitement. That's right, I had it bad, to say the least. I grabbed that letter, shut my mailbox, ran to the first bench outside the Student Center, and opened and read the letter. Then I read every word while imagining her face saying all these things to me. As I said, I had it bad. But to read it once was not enough. I had to reread it to ensure I didn't miss anything. Then I put the note in my pants pocket and headed back to my dorm. When I got back to the dorm, I would read it repeatedly. I studied that letter. I meditated on that letter. Before I received the following one, I had this letter memorized. No joke.

Deuteronomy 6:6-7 says, "These commandments that I give you today are to be upon your hearts. Impress them on your children. Talk about them when you sit at home and when you walk along the road, when you lie down and when you get up. Tie them as symbols on your hands and bind them on your foreheads. Write them on the doorframes of your house and on your gates."

God has written us a love letter from Heaven. He has filled it with some incredible truths and directions for life. His love letter is called the Bible, God's Holy Word. In his love letter to us, He shows us his grace and mercy. He tells us how to live life with joy, fulfillment, and peace. He shares incredible truths about how to overcome worries, disappointment, and stress. He tells us that He will never leave us or forsake us no matter what. And in his love letter, He also tells us how much He loves us and what he did to prove that to us. Yes, it took the time and energy to put this love letter together just for you and me. What an awesome God we serve.

Do you embrace His Word? Do you hinge on every word? Do you read it repeatedly? Do you meditate on God's Word night and day? Do you carry it around with you everywhere you go? Do you memorize it? Has this love letter changed your life?

Psalm 119:9-11: "How can a young man keep his way pure? By living according to your word. I seek you with all my heart; do not let me stray from your commands. I have hidden your word in my heart that I might not sin against you."

Know this. The Word of God is profitable, and when you read it, it will change you. How?

1. The Word of God helps you to resist temptation.

Matthew 4:1-3: "Then Jesus was led by the Spirit into the desert to be tempted by the devil. After fasting forty days and 40 nights, he was hungry. The tempter came to him and said, "If you are the Son of God, tell these stones to become bread."

There was no doubt that Jesus had to be physically weak from not eating for 40 days. If I don't eat every six hours, I get grumpy. How about you? Here is what I want you to notice; even though Jesus was weak physically, He was strong spiritually because he had been feasting on the Word of God. He had spiritual food stored up. Look how Jesus responded to the Devil's temptation in Matthew 4:4: "Jesus answered:

"It is written: Man does not live on bread alone, but on every word that comes from the mouth of God."

Jesus overcame the temptation of Satan by using scripture. Satan failed to get Jesus to fall into sin, but He never gave up. Twice more, Satan tempted Jesus with lies and deceit, but Jesus returned to the scriptures and trusted God's Holy Word. Hide God's Word in your heart.

2. The Word of God fills your mind with God.

What are you consuming? What are you watching and listening to? What are you filling your mind with? Have you ever stopped to think about all the information you take in daily? Our brain never turns off, even when we sleep. We are overloaded when it comes to data. We fill our minds with all sorts of useless information every minute of the day. Think about it, in our society today, we are always looking at our computers or phones. We are scrolling on Facebook and Instagram. We are checking out what people are doing all over the world. I don't know about you, but my mind is like my old phone. It only has so much memory.

I receive messages almost daily about buying more memory where I can add more pictures or store more information. What should I do? I start deleting old videos and photos because I am cheap. In the same way, our minds are so full of the things of this world that there is no room for God's Word. Garbage in, garbage out. It's time to delete those things that weigh us down. It's time to delete the useless information and lies Satan gives us. For many of us, we must delete a lot of trash to make room for truth. Take in God's Word daily. Consume, digest, and memorize the Word, and let it take over your mind.

THE TOTAL PACKAGE

3. The Word of God enables the Holy Spirit to teach and guide you in daily living.

Psalm 119:105 says, "Your word is a lamp to my feet and a light for my path."

Thank goodness for the gift of the Holy Spirit. We have a promise from God above that He would never leave or forsake us, and He promised that He would send us a helper, the Holy Spirit, to everyone who follows Christ.

I hate to admit this, but I am not one who always follows instructions well. Is anybody with me? I know many men who are the same way. How many of us ever had a new piece of furniture that you had to put together? It required some assembly. Have you ever opened a box, poured out all the pieces on the floor, stood over it, and said, "This is going to take forever?" This assembly is going to be two hours of my life that are wasted. I don't mean to be negative, but that was how I felt. As I sort through all the pieces and organize everything into different piles, I envision how the piece of furniture is supposed to look once I'm finished. I notice a couple of pieces of paper lying on the floor, but I kind of push those to the side. Who needs instructions? I got this, and I can do it faster my way. So, I think.

I get started. I begin to construct my piece of furniture. Everything is going smoothly, and it's not taking as long as I thought. As the project was coming to completion, I ran into a sag. Something was wrong. It was not lining up right. I became agitated, and I was losing valuable time. Where did I go wrong? My wife noticed my frustration and asked, "What's wrong?" I began to go through the whole process out loud. I also voiced my frustration to her in the entirety. By this time, I was tired, super frustrated, and aggravated. My wife walked over, picked up the instructions off the floor, handed them to me, and said, "You might want to read this." That was not what I wanted to hear at the time, but it was the truth I needed to hear. I had to slow down and take my time to read the instructions. I ended up taking most of it apart and followed the directions step-by-step. I was amazed at how fast and easy it was to put together when I followed the instructions.

God's Word is the instruction book on how to build a life of joy and true peace. It gives us step-by-step instructions on how to live life, raise a family, raise God-honoring children, how we are to handle difficult situations, and how we become a person who honors Him with our lives. I want to encourage you to slow down and take time to read God's instruction book and follow it step-by-step. It will save you a lot of headaches along the way. We need God's Word in our lives. We must give God's Word priority in our lives. Allow the Holy Spirit inside you to guide you through all the truths. God's Word in and God's Word out. Let the reality of the Bible flow through your life.

I have been in ministry for over 30 years now. I will be the first to say it's not always a bed of roses. I have made some mistakes along the way and have some regrets. I have been hurt, disappointed, and worn out. There have been times when I felt like I was wasting my time and just going through the motions of ministry. However, the good surely has outweighed the bad. As I look back and reflect on ministry, family, and friends, there is one thing that keeps me on the road. When the storm winds are blowing, and the waves of life are crashing around me, God's Word and my time alone with Him are what hold me steady. He is my rock, my fortress, and my high tower.

THE TOTAL PACKAGE

Jesus grew in favor with God. Are you growing in Him? Open His instruction book and dig in. Take time to dig for the treasures God wants to give you. Grow in your walk with the Father by communicating openly by talking and listening to what He has to say to you. Be obedient to what He tells you. Pay attention to the littlest details and allow Him to work freely in your life.

Chapter 13
Accountability

Luke 2:52 And Jesus increased in wisdom and in stature and in favor with God and man.

Proverbs 27:17 says, "As iron sharpens iron, so one man sharpens another."

Ecclesiastes 4:9-10: "Two are better than one, because they have a good return for their work: If one falls down, his friend can help him up. But pity the man who falls and has no one to help him up!"

We all need help and accountability. We need each other. There is only so much we can do on our own. I don't know about you, but I need encouragement. There is a limit to what discipline and passion can accomplish. We all face discouragement and challenging times in this life. Being a Christian and living a life of faith is like being in a boxing ring with a powerful opponent. It is a battle. If you are in Christ, our opponent is Satan himself.

John 10:10: "The thief comes to kill, steal, and destroy."

He never gives up, and he doesn't fight fair at all. We are fighting a spiritual war. You may have taken a couple of good licks from Satan, and he may have dazed you well, but you must keep fighting. There will be times when you feel like you are just hanging on to get to the bell. My question is this, who is in your corner? Who is your coach? Where is the motivation coming from in your corner? Think about it this way. A professional fighter doesn't do it alone. He surrounds himself with people who can make him better. He surrounds himself with people who have experience and knows what is going on. The boxer needs people who have been there and done that. That boxer needs people around him who know his weaknesses but, more importantly, know how to make him stronger. Yes, we need people who will push us and people who will be brutally honest with us. We need people around us who care for us and motivate us to keep fighting.

Who is in your corner? Who has been there and done that? Who is that person that motivates you? Who is there to encourage and support you? I love to get people thinking by asking questions. I love to see people working things through in their minds and processing how that would look in their lives. I want to ask you four simple questions that have to do with accountability.

1. Why should you be accountable to someone?

It's scriptural! It is encouraged and supported in God's Word.

Ephesians 5:21: "Summit to one another out of reverence for Christ."

Galatians 6:2: "Carry each other's burdens, and this way you will fulfill the law of Christ."

2 Timothy 2:22: "Flee the evil desires of youth, and pursue righteousness, faith, love and peace, along with people who call on the Lord out of a pure heart."

Accountability protects you from Satan and helps you build a pure life. As believers in Christ, we are to submit to one another and help to carry each other's burdens of life.

Romans 14:12: "So, then, each of us will give an account of himself in God."

Because I will have to give an account of my entire life to God, I need to use every means possible to live a godly life. Accountability works. Our flesh is weak. How often have we started with good intentions and, over time, fell flat on our faces? If we go on this journey alone, we will have only ourselves to answer to. But we double our accountability if we tell someone else what we are committing to.

I have been trying to write this book for several years. This desire is something I wanted to do, but I kept it all to myself. Time passed, I got busy doing other things, and I lost focus. I never got around to it. Over the last couple of months, I told family and a few friends what I wanted to do. Then I shared it with my church family. Now it is out there, and I have some accountability. And I now have people who are asking how my writing is going. So, I have had to up my game. I had to set aside extra time to see this thing through and dig deeper into my thoughts. Again, accountability works.

This point leads to my second question that has to do with accountability:

2. If accountability works, why do you refuse to have an accountability partner?

THE TOTAL PACKAGE

The number one reason you do not want someone to hold you accountable is because of selfish pride.

Proverbs 16:18-19 says this, "Pride goes before destruction, a haughty spirit before a fall. Better to be lowly in spirit and among the oppressed than to share plunder with the proud."

We are sometimes too proud to let down our guard or to take off our spiritual masks. We need to drop the pretense and be willing to share the real me. The second reason we shy away from getting an accountability partner is we lack commitment. We fear what it may cost us. We begin to wonder what we will have to give up going all in with Christ. The third reason we don't want someone in our corner is fear. Many of us are afraid that someone will get to know the real me. They would find out all my weaknesses and issues and then would never look at me the same again. The fourth reason we never took the time to get some accountability is we are just flat lazy. Sometimes in our lives, we just don't care and don't want anybody in our face. Our want to has got up and left the building.

3. What type of person should be your Corner Man?

Proverbs 13:20: "He who walks with the wise grows wise, but a companion of fools suffers harm."

You need someone in your corner that has been where you are at in life. You need someone who has been through the fires of life and has passed the tests. Someone that is mature in their faith and grounded in the Word of God. You need someone in your life that doesn't mind calling you out and willing to ask you difficult questions. But most of all, you need someone who will love you through the thick and the thin. I ask you again, who is in your corner?

    4. What needs to happen with your accountability partner?

First, take time to get to know each other and ask each other questions about life and faith. Then look at your life, see where you are, and talk about where you want to go. Establish some goals, both short-term and long-term goals. Look at what James 5:16 says,

"Therefore, confess your sins to each other and pray for each other so that you may be healed. The prayer of a righteous man is powerful and effective."

Yes, you need to pray with each other and pray for one other. You need to be willing to be open and honest with each other. Finally, accountability partners must encourage and challenge one another in our faith.

I urge you to get involved in a Bible-believing local body of believers. We all need to sit under the teachings of God's Holy Word and be engaged in some form of a small group. We all need encouragement and support to grow in a way that pleases God. It is good to do life together because God didn't design us to do it alone. Also, begin to pray for that person who could be that accountability partner for you. Then keep your spiritual eyes and ears open to what God has for you.

Chapter 14
March Down the Field

Luke 2:52 And Jesus increased in wisdom and in stature and in favor with God and man.

I want to take you back to the fall of 1985 and my senior year at Dougherty High School in Albany, Georgia. It is Friday night and time for some high school football. In my senior year, I played both sides of the ball, and the only time I came off the field was on the punt return. Yes, I had a ton of fun, but we ended up 1-9 that year. I was on the kickoff receiving team, and I still remember the excitement at the beginning of the game. There was the anticipation of how good the other team would be, how hard they would hit me, and if we could follow through with the game plan. The band was playing, and the crowd was cheering, and I remember the nervous jitters deep in my gut. The referees then would blow the whistle to begin the game. This was Friday night football in Southwest Georgia.

The other team kicked the ball off and proceeded to tear down the field. I wasn't the deep man on the kickoff because I didn't have great speed. But I was the one just to his right. I never had a ball come to me all season, which was fine. But things were about to change. I remember it like it was yesterday. That very first kick-off to start the game was coming straight to me. You've got to be kidding. I remember feeling great fear and praying that I wouldn't drop the ball. In an instance, the band noise disappeared, and I couldn't hear the crowd noise any longer. There was total silence in my mind. All I remember was seeing the football in that

South Georgia black sky. I was so focused on that ball that nothing else mattered. I remember thinking in my mind, don't drop the ball. No matter what, don't drop the ball.

As the ball came down, I gathered my nerves and positioned myself to catch this football. I was focused, and my eyes didn't leave that ball. My heart was pounding, and my mind was racing. It seemed like the ball would never come down at that moment as it tumbled end over end. Still, I didn't hear anything around me. Then I caught the ball. Yes! Then it was like someone turned up the volume of life. I began to hear the grunts of people getting hit, and I remember the bodies flying around me. The band was blaring, and the crowd yelled, "run!" So, I took off and avoided one tackle, but all I could get was about ten yards on the return before getting hammered. After that first hit, everything began to slow down, and the excitement and the adrenaline weren't raging. We had the ball on the 30-yard line, and we had to march down the field 70 yards. All the hype and excitement were gone, and now we had to grind it out. We had to join as a team and push through difficulty and opposition to reach our goal.

I remember receiving Christ as my Lord and Savior. I remember the excitement, butterflies, and all the "amens." I felt like nothing else mattered at that point and time in my life. I was so in love with God and couldn't wait to tell my friends. I was so attuned to the Father that I didn't even hear the noise of the crowd. But then life happened, and the noise of the world returned, and the game of life moved on. This reality is where the rubber meets the road, and you must live out your faith and overcome sin and temptations. I want to give you three steps to remember that will help you walk out your faith daily.

THE TOTAL PACKAGE

1. Trust the game plan.

Choose to dwell on the truth. We must put into practice what we know as truth. We must follow the game plan that is laid out for us in the playbook. We know that as God's Word. I will go ahead and tell you it's not going to be easy. You will be hit on every side and may get hurt along the way, but you must push through. You must stay focused, and you need to stay the course. You must know in your heart that this is the best way. Have faith in your coach. Preparation is so necessary. Hang on to the truth you discovered in your walk with Christ. Expose the devil's lies and replace them with the truth. Let prayer be your release of worry and doubt while giving God your fears and your dreams. Take time to listen to His voice of comfort and peace. Receive His instructions for life and His game plan for ministry. Have confidence in the preparations and dwell in His amazing love and grace. He promises us that He will never leave you or forsake you. Yes, you may face great hardship and difficulties in this life, but you have a Heavenly Father that will calm the seas and provide strength to get through the storm.

Proverbs 3:5-6: "Trust in the Lord with all your heart and lean not on your own understanding; in all your ways acknowledge him, and he will make your paths straight."

2. Shut out the noise.

In 1985, Central Thomasville was a state power in Georgia High School football. We knew going into the game that it would be a beat down. Their two best players were their defensive ends. They both were big, strong, and very athletic. I was running from them all night. If I got away from one, the other one would hit me from the other side. But what threw me off was the endless chatter that never stopped. To say the least, they were in my head. Instead of focusing on my job and what I had to do, I was listening to the voices of my opponent. I was setting myself up for failure. They hit me so many times that night I lost track of how many sacks I fell to.

How often do we allow our opponent, "The Devil" to trash-talk us and fill our lives with fear and doubt? Shut out the noise of this world.

- What does that look like for you?
- What do you fill your mind with?
- What voices are you listening to?

It is so easy to get distracted and get off track by listening to the noise of this world. Mary and Martha were good friends of Jesus. He went to their home just to sit down and visit them. When Jesus arrived, Martha was distracted by all the preparations. She wanted everything to be perfect for Jesus. Martha was flying all over the house, trying to get everything done, but Mary decided to sit at the feet of Jesus and catch up. She just wanted to talk and fellowship with her friend Jesus. This devotion made Martha very upset. She was so frustrated she stopped working and asked Jesus, "Don't you care that Mary is doing nothing to help me with all this work?" Jesus replied in Luke 10: 41-42:

"Martha, Martha,' the Lord answered, 'you are worried and upset about many things, but only one thing is needed. Mary has chosen what is better, and it will not be taken from her.'"

3. Find the first down marker.

THE TOTAL PACKAGE

That football game is forever etched in my mind. That night 70 yards seemed impossible to reach. My goal that night wasn't to get a touchdown but just get to the first down marker and go from there. There is only one way to eat an elephant, one bite at a time. Walking out of the Christian life can be difficult at times but set up some short-term goals and go after those first down markers. Yes, even celebrate those small victories. There will be days when you oversleep or run late for work and miss your time alone with God. There will be days when you get sacked and even fumble the ball. Don't be overwhelmed or discouraged. Keep your eyes on the first down marker and listen to the Coach's voice.

Hebrews 12:2-3: "Let us fix our eyes on Jesus, the author and perfecter of our faith, who for the joy set before him endured the cross, scorning its shame, and sat down at the right hand of the throne of God. Consider him who endured such opposition from sinful men, so that you will not grow weary and lose heart."

4. You don't have to do it alone.

Sometimes in the intensity of that game with Thomasville Central, I felt isolated and alone. For some reason, I felt like it was a battle between them and me. I was so focused on them and their position on the field that I almost forgot there were ten others on my team that was fighting with me. We don't have to do it alone. God has surrounded us with people that will encourage, equip, and support us. Plus, He has given us a Helper. If you are a child of God, He has given you the gift of the Holy Spirit.

John 14:15-18: "If you love me, you will do what I command. And I will ask the Father, and he will give you another Counselor to be with you forever- the Spirit of truth. The world cannot accept him, because it neither sees him nor knows him. But you know him, for he lives with you and will be in you. I will not leave you as orphans; I will come to you."

Grow in favor with God. Break down the walls of selfishness, pride, and sin. Lay a good foundation found only in a personal relationship with Jesus Christ. Then build on that foundation through your time alone with your loving heavenly Father. Spend time in His Word and cover everything you do in prayer. Make sure you have some accountability partners in place that will be by your side and get involved with a local body of Bible-believing Christians. Then march down that field. Watch out for Satan's schemes and tricks. He will hit you from your blindside and won't feel bad for doing it. Keep your eyes on that first down marker. Set up some short-term goals and stay focused on Jesus. The Christian life is not a sprint but a marathon. Stay at it and never give up.

God's best is still in front of you!

Section 4:
Jesus Grew
In Favor With Man

Chapter 15
Relationships

Luke 2:52 And Jesus increased in wisdom and in stature and in favor with God and man.

One thing is for sure when it comes to relationships; you will not always agree. There will come a time in every relationship when you face conflict. How will you respond in the face of this conflict? What will you say when you get to your boiling point? When you face adversity in your life, do you run and hide and shut everyone out, or do you lash out and blurt out the first thing that comes to mind?

One of my favorite toys growing up was a cork-loaded air rifle. I remember playing Cowboys and Indians and having the time of my life with that gun. I didn't want to put the gun down many nights, so I carried it to bed and held it all night. It was my constant friend. In my eyes, it looked just like a real gun except for the cork on the end. I could cock the gun, point it at my target, and shoot. Then the cork would pop off the end of my air rifle. The greatest thing about my gun was the cork was attached to a string. So, every time I pulled the trigger, the cork would pop off, the string would catch it, and then I would push it back into the end of the gun for another shot.

Don't you wish your words had a string where you could pull them back when you pop off at the mouth? Do you ever wish you could go back and do something all over again? Have you ever spoken words out of anger that you wished you had a string attached to the end? Have you ever tried to be funny and ended up hurting someone's feelings? You didn't mean to insult them or belittle them. Have you ever put your foot in your mouth or wished you could dig a hole and hide in it?

I remember holding a conversation with a lady friend of mine. We were friends, but I didn't know her that well. She had been married for a couple of years, and I noticed she had added a little weight. It looked like she had a baby bump. I proceeded to say, "How far along are you?" Her facial expression began to change instantly, and she responded, "Excuse me, I am not pregnant." She took it like a champ, but I wished I had a string to pull back those words. She was laughing on the outside, but those words probably hurt her feelings. Even though I didn't mean any harm, they still hurt.

Let me tell you this, some of the most hurtful situations have happened in the church. I can tell you story after story of all the arguments I have heard growing up in the church. It is sad to say, but I am speaking the truth. In my lifetime, I have seen some outrageous business meetings. Yes, there will be differences of opinion, fussing, and fighting, but no throwing hands. I have seen families voted out of the church. I have been a part of churches when they asked their pastor to leave, which is never a pleasant time in the life of a church. People begin to take sides, and, of course, everyone has their own opinion of what is right and wrong.

I have sat through some heated discussions about what carpet looks the best in the sanctuary or what color would look best on the new bus. I could tell you about church arguments, and it would probably be very entertaining. I am sure you have some stories of your own that haunt your mind.

I have said all this to say that we all have broken relationships that we must deal with for healing. If you are involved in ministry long enough, there will be challenging times when it comes to relationships. There will be those who believe you are doing it all wrong or have a strong opinion of how it should be done. Be aware of those who are friendly to your face but talk about you when your back is turned. Have you ever been there? How do we respond to these kinds of toxic relationships?

1. We try to push the issues under the rug or push them aside like it is no big deal.

We may even deny there is a problem. So, we try our best to avoid the issues, but they always seem to keep popping up. God has a funny sense of humor at times. Have you ever noticed that when troubled relationships are left alone, they grow worse and even more toxic, just like a fungus? But you continue to say, "It's no big deal. It will work itself out." Then you continue with life. Think about your real-life encounters. What friends are popping up in your mind as you read this? God is pushing them in front of you for a reason. What relationship issues have you swept under the rug or moved to the side? It's incredible how you can be so mad at someone for so long and forget why you were mad at them in the first place. Have you ever stopped long enough to realize what blessings you miss out on because of that broken relationship?

Ephesians 4:26-27: "In your anger so not sin": Do not let the sun go down while you are still angry, and do not give the devil a foothold."

2. We try to present our case.

THE TOTAL PACKAGE

How many of you love watching the old TV show "Perry Mason?" He was an old-school lawyer who never lost a case. What about Ben Matlock, a country version of Perry Mason? Ben was a country lawyer who used his Southern charm and wit to lure you to sleep and swoop down every time to pull out a victory. Even today, one of my favorite shows is "Law and Order." I love how they dig into a case and investigate from every angle. They put so much time and effort into digging up dirt on the defendant and will use any form of information to put these people behind bars. In some cases, the lawyers become consumed with finding more evidence and information that affects their family life, sleeping habits, and demeanor.

Toxic relationships can consume you, and they have a way of taking over your life and exhausting all your energy. When you are upset and mad at someone that has wronged you or your family, your instinct is to jump back at them. I don't care how spiritual you are; something in you wants to defend yourself, especially your family. Not only will you protect yourself, but also you will dig into their life, find out all their dirt, and then proceed to present it to all of those around you. You must prove to others that you were right. You may even feel like you won your case or got the upper hand, but what did it cost you?

Ephesians 4:31-32: "Get rid of all bitterness, rage, and anger, brawling and slander, along with every form of malice. Be kind and compassionate to one another, forgiving each other, just as in Christ God forgave you."

3. The third way you deal with toxic relationships is to pretend that this relationship is no big deal and it's time to declare war.

Then you will put up a huge pretense that you can shut them out of your life and pretend that what they said about you didn't hurt and it was no big deal. Yes, you go past building your case against this person and trying your best to tear them down or discredit them. But there is so much pain, hurt, and hard feelings. You may believe it is past the point of ever restoring this relationship. Not only do you not like this person, but everyone around you also knows you don't like them. They see your pain, they have heard all the evidence, and some have even picked sides. Does this sound familiar? Have you ever been there?

Jesus speaks in Matthew 5:21-24, "You have heard that it was said to the people long ago, 'Do not murder, and anyone who murders will be subject to judgment.' But I tell you that anyone who is angry with his brother will be subject to judgment. Again, anyone who says to his brother, 'Raca,' is answerable to the Sanhedrin. But anyone who says, 'You fool!' will be in danger of the fire of hell. Therefore, if you are offering your gift at the altar and they remember that your brother has something against you, leave your gift there in front of the altar. First go and be reconciled to your brother; then come and offer your gift."

If you are a believer in Christ Jesus, He gave us specific instructions on dealing with toxic relationships. I want to bring out a couple of points that Jesus made here.

Jesus said, "Anyone who is angry with his brother will be subject to judgment." We are held accountable for our relationships with other people. Broken relationships are a big deal to God, so for us, they should also be a big deal. We can pretend to put up a huge front and act like it doesn't bother us. Or we can even declare an all-out war on that person. In either case, it is wrong in the sight of God because God calls that sin. And sin hinders our relationship with Him.

First, I want to encourage you to stop and listen to what the Father is saying about your relationships. Spend time to take inventory of all your relationships. Get a pen and paper, list all the different people in your life, and begin with those closest to you. One by one, ask yourself some questions about each person. Yes, this will take some time, but it will be worth it. Ask yourself these questions:
- What is my overall health in this relationship? (Scale of 1-10)
- Are there walls that need to come down?
- Are there things I need to talk through?
- Are there undiscussed hurts that I am hanging on to?
- Do I need to say, "I am sorry?"

As you pray to the Father and evaluate your relationships, God will put the situation, discussions, and events in front of you. Sometimes He will show you things you don't want to see about yourself. You can try your best to ignore the purple elephant in front of you, but God doesn't give up. You will keep leading in your church, teaching Sunday School, singing in the choir, and acting like nothing is wrong.

Second, leave your offering, leave your worship, leave your leadership at the altar, and go and make things right with your brother. In other words, stop the role-play and take care of business. Before you tell others about God's love, you must walk it out yourself. Some of the hardest things in life to do are to swallow your pride and say, "I am sorry," or "let's get things right." To be completely honest with you, sometimes I'd rather bite my tongue off than say those words. But in most cases, those words are the first steps to restoring a relationship and a beginning of the moving of the Holy Spirit in your life.

Third, in Matthew 5:25, Jesus said, "Settle matters quickly!" Settling matters of the heart quickly is so essential when it comes to restoring relationships. The longer you wait and hold onto a grudge, the harder it is to make things right.

This next story is a crazy illustration, but here you go. I love to drink coffee. Every morning I get up and make a pot of coffee. It is part of my daily routine. Laura and I have a very honest relationship with each other, and we can say almost anything to each other. It hasn't always been this way, but after 35 years of marriage, we have learned to overlook some things. One day, out of the blue, Laura said, "You might want to do something about your teeth." I stepped back and said, "What are you talking about?" She responded, "You are getting old man teeth; they look stained."

To be honest with you, that hurt my feelings. Of course, I played it off and acted like it was no big deal. A few days later, I just happened to go to the dentist. After they cleaned my teeth, I asked, "What can I do about my coffee-stained teeth?" Of course, the first option was to get their $1000.00 whiting treatment. I squashed that option right then and there! There was no way I would pay anybody $1000.00 to make my teeth whiter. So, now she began encouraging me to brush my teeth right after I drank coffee or at least rinse my mouth with water. She also told me about some whitening strips and mouthwashes that would do a good job but not as good as the $1000.00 treatment. The last thing she told me was this, "The longer the coffee sits on your teeth, the darker the stains will be."

For some, you have harbored unforgiveness, hate, and bitterness for so long that you don't know what it feels like to live a life any other way. It has been with you so long; you have become stained. You have lost hope of ever getting things right. You have given up on restoration and written that person off. I have one verse for you to pray.

Matthew 19:26 Jesus said, "With man this is impossible, but with God all things are possible."

It's never too late. Don't let those wounds and disappointments build up and fester. Be direct, open, and honest with those people you care about. Don't give Satan the victory. God is calling you to make things right today. Don't put it off.

Chapter 16
Choose Your Words Wisely

Luke 2:52 And Jesus increased in wisdom and in stature and in favor with God and man.

The Apostle Peter said through the inspiration of the Holy Spirit, "Be holy, for I am holy." That was a command of God in 1 Peter 1:16. How intimidating is that statement? The Bible is full of instructions to become more like Christ in every area of our life. Our goal should be to become that "Total Package," just like Jesus. I believe this last section of growing in favor with man could be the most difficult. The first three sections mainly have to do with yourself and God. We know ourselves well. We know our weaknesses, struggles, and our strengths. We also know where God stands and what He is all about. God never waivers; He is the same yesterday, today, and forever. I also know that I need to adapt and change to become more and more like Jesus. He lived the perfect life, so Jesus is much easier to love, honor, and respect. But dealing with imperfect people can be tricky and very frustrating, to say the least. Our responses to difficult people and awkward situations tell a lot about our true selves. To grow in favor with man is learning how to relate to people as Jesus did.

As I studied the life of Jesus, He had to make certain choices. He chose to encourage. He chose to forgive and to love. Yes, He lived in a world much like ours today, where there was hatred, jealousy, envy, strife, and injustice. But He was without sin and handled difficult situations with God's grace and wisdom. He was faced with conflict and a crisis. But in every way, He pleased the Father. In this crazy world of sickness and strife, Jesus chose to speak the truth, not just words people wanted to hear. Take Jesus' most famous sermon of all times, the Sermon on the Mount.

In Matthew 5:1-2, Jesus saw the crowds and went to the mountainside and sat down and began to teach. In verses 3-12 Jesus said, "Blessed are the poor in spirit, for theirs is the kingdom of heaven. Blessed are those who mourn, for they will be comforted. Blessed are the meek, for they will inherit the earth. Blessed are those who hunger and thirst for righteousness, for they will be filled. Blessed are the merciful, for they will be shown mercy. Blessed are the pure in heart, for they will see God. Blessed are the peacemakers, for they will be called sons of God. Blessed are those who are persecuted because of righteousness, for theirs is the kingdom of heaven. Blessed are you when people insult you, persecute you and falsely say all kinds of evil against you because of me. Rejoice and be glad, because great is your reward in heaven, for in the same way they persecuted the prophets who were before you."

Speak words of truth. Jesus shared the truth. He didn't use words of flattery or deceit. How many people would leave the church if Jesus were their pastor in America today? Who in their right mind would want to hear a sermon on becoming meek and humble, being a peacemaker, and being ok to be persecuted? In Jesus' day, the children of God were under the rule of Rome, and they were oppressed. Wouldn't you think the people wanted to hear a message about victory, overcoming, and prosperity? Jesus didn't put up a front. He was committed to his calling.

He didn't speak words to gain an advantage in business or to make more money.

Matthew 5:20 Where Jesus said, "For I tell you that unless your righteousness surpasses that of the Pharisees and the teachers of the law, you will certainly not enter the kingdom of heaven."

Wow, such strong words. When I read God's Word, I try to put myself there with Jesus. I try to picture His face and His expressions. I try to imagine the surroundings. I try hard to imagine how different people would respond to His words. I think in this moment and time, Jesus hit a very touchy spot. He could have easily not mentioned all this so early in His ministry, and it would have probably saved Him a headache for the next several years. This sermon most likely didn't sit well with some of the religious leaders of the day. They were not used to hearing the truth or having someone correct them. Jesus chose to speak the truth and not lie. It is better to be divided by truth than to be united in error. In other words, it is better to speak the truth that hurts and heals than to share lies that comfort and heal. Jesus was just getting started. He goes on to speak about broken relationships and settling matters quickly, as we mentioned in the last chapter. He also talked about adultery and lust in the heart of man.

In Matthew 5:27-28, Jesus said, "You have heard that it was said, "Do not commit adultery." But I tell you that anyone who looks at a woman lustfully has already committed adultery with her in his heart."

Jesus is on a roll; he keeps the truth rolling in Matthew 5:44 and says:

THE TOTAL PACKAGE

"Love your enemies and pray for those who persecute you."

     To grow in our relationships, we need to speak words of truth. A good friend that cares about you and is concerned about the direction you are headed will not use words of flattery just to get on your good side. We need those friends that will speak truth into our lives and not be afraid to hold us accountable for how we live our lives. We need those people in our lives who don't always go along with every little idea we have. Yes, we need someone who loves us enough to be honest with us and sometimes is willing to push back. Speaking words of truth isn't always easy. Being upfront with someone can be challenging at times.

     Have you ever had that friend who thought they could sing? They were going to light the world on fire with their talent. They were always the loudest voice in the choir, and you could tell they were proud to share their talent with you. But if the truth is said, they can't sing a lick. They are tone death. Somehow and in some way, we need to be willing to say, "You are not on the pitch. Have you ever tried to play the guitar?"

In Matthew 7:13-14, Jesus said, "Enter through the narrow gate. For wide is the gate and broad is the way is the road that leads to destruction, and many will enter through it. But small is the gate and narrow the road that leads to life, and only a few will find it."

     That couldn't have been a popular message to the people of Jesus' day. That message could have cost Him losing members in His Church, so to speak. But Jesus didn't hold back the truth because it was uncomfortable or a problematic message to give.

He pressed on in Matthew 7:21-23 when he said, "Not everyone who says to me, "Lord, Lord." will enter the kingdom of heaven, but only he who does the will of my Father who is in heaven. Many will say to me on that day, "Lord, Lord, did we not prophesy in your name, and in your name drive out demons and perform many miracles?" Then I will tell them plainly, "I never knew you. Away from me, you evildoers."

These are hard words to hear, but Jesus spoke the truth. Sharing truth is not always easy, but it is necessary. Jesus also spoke words of hope. Look at the words of Jesus in John 3:16. Jesus says:

"For God so loved the world that he gave his one and only Son, that whoever believes in him shall not perish but have eternal life."

This verse must be the most memorized in the entire Bible. Hope is dripping off these words of Jesus. Some 2000 years later, these words are still bringing us hope today. It promises hope and a future because of what Jesus did for us. This verse spoke of God's amazing love for us even when we didn't deserve it. Jesus willingly paid the price to give us life and life more abundant. "Thank you, Lord!"

Growing up on the east side of Albany, Georgia, was a blessing. I was raised by two Godly parents. We were not rich by any means, and we surely didn't live in a fancy big house. I grew up in a Jim Walter home. In other words, this builder would build you a house up to 80% finished, and you would complete the additional 20% on your own. We

THE TOTAL PACKAGE

lived at 3220 Staton Drive, and life was good. My dad worked at the Marine Base, and my mom worked at a bank once we started school. We didn't have a lot, but we never realized it. My childhood was full of joy, happiness, and many great memories. I have many fond memories of playing ball in our backyard with our neighborhood friends and then joining a little league team.

At the age of nine, I went to try out, and all the coaches for all the minor league and major league teams were there watching. After the tryout, the Major League Cubs chose me. Over the next three years, we only lost three games. Football was a different story. I remember going to the recreation department to sign up. I was really excited to get all my pads. I will never forget the smell of that gym. Now all I needed to do was go to the local sporting goods store to get a helmet. The whole family piled in the car to head to Owen's Sporting Goods downtown Albany, Georgia. We pulled up, and it didn't take me long to pick out the perfect helmet. I wore that helmet like it was a crown. Of course, we had to rush back home to put it all on. Let me tell you, I felt indestructible, and I thought I could conquer the world. That year, the mighty Blue Jays were 0-6. We didn't win a game, but I had a lot of fun and looked good.

Other childhood memories included riding bikes all over creation, building and jumping ramps, hanging out with friends, building tree houses, and forts in the woods. My brother and I did everything together; we hunted birds with our Red Rider BB gun. We didn't kill too many birds until we graduated with our new 880 pump air rifle. It was awesome. We could pump that gun up about ten times and kill every bird we hit. Let me tell you. We were the "big dogs" and the talk of the neighborhood. We quickly dropped the bike when we got our first motorcycle. My brother and I never had our own motorcycle, so we had to share. So, we devised a plan. We would do so many laps or go and ride in the woods for so many minutes, but we had to be back at a specific time. If we rode a couple of hours Monday, Tuesday, and Wednesday and used all the gas, then we wouldn't get to ride again till next week. We were on a budget. I remember running out of gas several times and having to push that motorcycle back home from the woods. I could go on and on about my childhood and how good life was.

But I want to fast forward to my 10th-grade year of high school. Yes, I was still playing football, basketball, and baseball. Our JV team was undefeated, and we were destroying everybody. I threw for over 200 yards in every game. I had a beautiful girlfriend who is now my wife of 35 years. I had my own car, which was huge for a guy raised in East Albany. At the time, it was everything I ever hoped life could be. It was what I called the perfect life.

But the pressures of life became real to me for the very first time. Sports weren't something I did for fun any longer, but it became a constant pressure to perform. I had to play every game at a certain level, and stats became much more important. People began talking about college and asking where I was going. I just started driving and found new freedom; with that new freedom, more choices had to be made. Up to this point in life, life was easy. I never had to study and always made A s and B s, which was fine for me. I got caught up in the hype of being the starting quarterback and the starting pitcher on the baseball diamond. But as the pressures built up, my world started falling apart. My grades began to slip, and I made two Fs as my final grade for the first time in my life. It felt like a nightmare, and I couldn't wake myself up. I remember sitting in my bedroom of our Jim Walter Home feeling confused, frustrated, overwhelmed, defeated, and tired. Everybody thought I had it all together. Boy, did I have them fooled? All I wanted to do was sit in my room and have a huge pity party. I tried to shut the world out.

But God knew exactly what I needed. He sent my mom to me that day. Yes, I had to dump a whole lot of baggage on her that day. I complained about life and how sorry the teachers were at Dougherty High School. I thought life, as I knew it was over, and there was no recovery from all of this. My mom listened to every complaint and didn't interrupt me one time. I mean, I threw up on her good. As I wrapped up my whining session, she came and sat down with me on my bed, and without saying a word, she gave me the biggest hug a son could ever hope for. How did she know exactly what I needed? Then after that incredible hug, she looked me in the eyes and said, "I love you." She spoke words of wisdom, and I listened. She spoke words of hope and encouragement over me. She told me that day that God had a unique plan for me, and I needed to press through the hard times. She assured me that God would use this difficult time in my life to make me stronger and become the man He was calling me to be.

We need truth spoken into our lives, and we need people who will get in our faces. But we also need to hear words of hope from those closest to us. Those words of hope pushed me and encouraged me to press on through those difficult times. Those simple words have changed my life forever.

As we build relationships and grow in favor with men, be that voice of encouragement that brings hope back to people's lives. It is hard to stay positive in a hostile world, but I am convinced everyone has some good. We may have to dig a little in some people's life to find it, but it's there. Be that voice of hope. Jesus spoke words of truth, of hope, and He walked it out with love. Then He changed the world.

Jesus spoke these words in John 13:34-35, "A new commandment I give you: Love one another. As I have loved you, so you must love one another. By this all men will know that you are my disciples if you love one another."

It is so good to hear words of encouragement and words of affirmation. I appreciate those people in my life who speak the truth over me. We all need that in our lives. "Thank you, Lord, for those you have placed around me who love me and are willing to put their love into action."

THE TOTAL PACKAGE

Chapter 17
Put Love into Action

Luke 2:52 And Jesus increased in wisdom and in stature and in favor with God and man.

To win with people, you must love the way Jesus loved. Encouraging words are good, but actions speak louder than words. What is your life screaming to the world? What message are you sharing with those around you at work, on the ball field, and even in church? Are you truly living out what you believe? My former pastor talked to me about ministry. He told me that too many people want to make ministry too complicated. He said it comes down to two things; you must love God and people. He told me, "If I can do that, I would do well in ministry."

In John 4:3-6, the author tells us that Jesus was leaving Judea and returning to Galilee. Then John tells us He went through Samaria and met the woman there at the well. Jesus always went out of His way to minister to people and share the Good News. I don't know about you, but I don't want to make unnecessary stops when I go on a trip. I remember traveling with my girls when they were young, and we would drive to the beach for a couple of days. It was close to a three-and-a-half-hour trip. Mackenzie, my youngest daughter, was constantly thirsty and always asked for her apple juice, and my wife always gave in. Then 40 minutes down the road, Mackenzie would say, "I've got to go to the bathroom!" It would frustrate me to no end. These frequent stops were killing my travel time. With each stop, it would delay us another 20 minutes. Then I would have to put my foot down and say, "No more juice for you!" I was known as the "Juice Nazi."

This realization is hard to say, but sometimes it is good to slow down and enjoy life. You don't always have to be in a rush. Take time to open your eyes and see the things and the people around you. Yes, sometimes it is good to pull off the fast, busy highway and get on a dirt road. You will see things there that you will never see on the busy highway. Don't be so regimented and rushed that we miss out on the blessings of life. Jesus slowed down, and He took the time to speak in this woman's life, and He took time to love her when no one else would. Sometimes you miss out on some of life's greatest miracles because you don't slow down to enjoy the things and people God places in front of you. Love how Jesus loved and be willing to give God your time to invest in people.

Jesus walked through this life with his eyes wide open. He tried to start conversations with strangers. He wasn't scared to ask them questions about their lives, and He honestly cared about what was going on with them. I love to hear people's stories. I love to hear about their life struggles and heartaches because we all have them. Too often, we want to tell our story and fill the internet with most of our life's greatest highlights and thrills. I love to brag about my girls; they are precious to me. They are my heartbeat. As a pastor, I am always in front of people. I am always sharing my story, life experiences, and my heartaches. But I must be willing to step out of the spotlight and take time to listen to the people's stories around me. We underestimate the ministry of listening, not saying a word or sharing our wisdom. We just need to sit back and listen to people's stories, hurts, and heartaches. Jesus could have

THE TOTAL PACKAGE

placed himself in the spotlight. He could have been this conquering king, and He could have ruled the world, and He could have been on every billboard in Israel. But He chose to meet with a prostitute at the well of some dusty road in Samaria. Most people wouldn't have given her the time of day, especially the religious people of his day, but Jesus cared enough to listen.

Matthew 9:35-36 says, "Jesus went through all the towns and villages, teaching in their synagogues, preaching the good news of the kingdom and healing every disease and sickness. When he saw the crowds, he had compassion on them, because they were harassed and helpless, like sheep without a shepherd."

Jesus wasn't stuck inside a building or at a specific address or location. His ministry extended far beyond a building. He went into the highways, byways, and even the dirt roads of life to love on people. Jesus' ministry was built on relationships. Yes, He spoke to the masses. Every time Jesus spoke, great crowds would follow. However, He did most of His work in very small groups as He invested in individual people. So, we know that Jesus went out of His way and sacrificed His time to love people. He also took time to listen to people's stories and cared enough to share the Good News with them. Let's look at the words of Jesus in John 4:21-26:

"Believe me, woman, a time is coming when you will worship the Father neither on this mountain nor in Jerusalem. You Samaritans worship what you do not see, for salvation is from the Jews. Yet a time is coming and has now come when the true worshipers will worship the Father in spirit and truth, for they are the kind of worshipers the Father seeks.

God is spirit, and his worshipers must worship in spirit and truth. The woman said, 'I know that the Messiah (called Christ) is coming. When he comes, he will explain everything to us.' Jesus declared, 'I who speak to you am he.'"

    Listen, I am not perfect, and I am just like everybody else. I mess up, and I have sin in my life. I fall short, but I have been set free, and I have a joy and peace that gives me hope and a passion for life. Yes, I have a reason to wake up every morning and a story to tell. I have a purpose in life, and it is all because of my love relationship with Jesus Christ. I remember as a child giving Christ my heart and asking for forgiveness and for Christ to cleanse me from sin. I believed He was God's Son and died on the old rugged cross. I also believe He is not in that grave and alive and well today. But most importantly, I know He lives in my heart. I remember at the age of five, asking Christ to sit on the throne of my heart, and I will never be the same again.

    He is my foundation and my cornerstone. He has held me close during the storms of life. He has been the glue that has kept my family and marriage together over these years. He was the one I leaned on when my health fell apart. That is the Good News in a nutshell, and I need to care enough about people to share what Jesus has done for me. Don't keep the greatest blessing of your life a secret, which is a relationship with Jesus Christ. Look at the woman at the well and her response to Jesus' investment.

John 4:28-29 said this, "Then, leaving her water jar, the woman went back to the town and said to the people, 'Come, see a man who told me everything I ever did, could this be Christ?' They came out of the town and made their way towards him."

THE TOTAL PACKAGE

Her life was changed forever, and it touched the lives of the community.

I want to encourage you to slow down enough to see the needs of others. Open your spiritual eyes to see those around you throughout your day. Take time to listen to their story and hear what their heart is saying. And don't be ashamed to share what God has done for you through a relationship with Jesus Christ.

There is another thing that Jesus did well that we need to emulate. He willingly served people. Jesus again is our ultimate example of being a servant leader. His heart was pure, and His motives were spotless. Jesus was the "Total Package" because he chose to serve others.

Philippians 2:5 tells us, "Your attitude should be the same as that of Christ Jesus."

In my opinion, I believe the greatest basketball player ever to play the game was Michael Jordan. I know people love to debate that, and they argue that it was LeBron James or Kobe Bryant. Everybody can have an opinion. Michael Jordan made a name for himself and put Nike on the map. He capitalized on his abilities, talents, and his giftings. His desire to win Championships was second to none, and he would do whatever it took to win. Yes, it was so much fun to watch him play on TV. He was a complete player. He could score with anybody in the league despite all the double teams. He was also one of the most dominating defensive players ever to play the game, and he knew how to play the game. In the process, he won six NBA World Championships. You mention Michael Jordan's name anywhere in the world, and people will know who you are talking about. Everyone wanted to be like Mike. You can say

Mike took a different route than Jesus. Michael cashed in on who he was, but Jesus chose to humble himself and took the role of a servant. Who are we most like, Mike or Jesus?

Philippians 2:6-7 says, "Who, being in very nature God, did not consider equality with God something to be grasped, but made himself nothing, taking the very nature of a servant, being made in human likeness."

Mike was looking out for himself. Jesus was looking out for us. Who is the true hero? Mike gave us shoes, and Jesus gave us eternal life. Because of that, I choose Jesus over Mike. You see, Jesus didn't just talk about being a servant leader. He led by example.

John 13:1-5 reads like this, "It was just before Passover Feast. Jesus knew that the time had come for him to leave this world and go to the Father. Having loved his own who were in the world, he showed them the full extent of his love. The evening meal was being served, and the devil had already prompted Judas Iscariot, son of Simon, to betray Jesus. Jesus knew that the Father had put all things under his power, and that he had come from God and was returning to God; so, he got up from the meal, took off his outer clothing, and wrapped a towel around his waist. After that, he poured water into the basin and began to wash his disciples' feet, drying them with the towel that was wrapped around him."

Jesus gave us a great example of how to serve people. Let's place ourselves into the culture of Jesus' day. There were no cars, bikes, and hardly any transportation as we know of today. So, the typical person walked everywhere. You also must remember this was way before Nike and Adidas existed, and they mostly wore open-toed sandals.

THE TOTAL PACKAGE

Now think about the type of roads they had to travel. There were no concrete walkways or paved roads. They mostly walked on the dirt and sand. Now picture their feet. Can you imagine the major toe jam?

It was the custom in Jesus' day that if you had guests over, you would have a servant wash their feet as they entered your home. That makes sense, right? I have a dog that stays inside, and her name is Miles. Let me get this straight, Miles is not my dog, but Miles lives at my house while my youngest daughter is off at school. I hate to admit what I am about to tell you, but it is true. When I let the dog out to take care of her business, her feet will be wiped off with a wet towel before she comes back in. That's right. I wash Mackenzie's dog's feet every day. I serve my dog daily. I understand this biblical custom. I wouldn't want some sandal-wearing, dirt-walking guy bringing dirt into my house. It makes sense to me. But it was more than that. The host would wash their guest's feet for their benefit. It was for the comfort and pleasure of their guest. For some unknown reason, the host of this get-together neglected to wash his guest's feet. What was this guy thinking? You had the great teacher and Messiah coming to your house, and you didn't have time to wash his feet? Even Jesus had toe-jam. But this opened the door for Jesus to give His disciples a learning moment, something that would stay with them for the rest of their lives.

In John 13:4, Jesus got up from the meal, took off his outer clothing, and wrapped a towel around His waist. My question to you is this. What do you have to get out of the way to serve people around you? For many "church people," pride must go. We can become so self-righteous, thinking we are too good to get ourselves dirty to put ourselves in a position of servant. Some may want the position with recognition and the position at the head of the table. Jesus was the leader and the great healer. He was also the one everyone came to hear teach. Yet, Jesus willingly served those who followed Him by washing away their toe jam. He was the coming King, yet He chose to serve those around him.

Look at John 13:13-15, "When he had finished washing the disciples' feet, he put on his clothes and returned to his place. 'Do you understand what I have done for you?' he asked them. 'You call me Teacher and Lord, and rightly so, for that is what I am. Now that I, your Lord, and Teacher, have washed your feet, you also should wash one another's feet. I have set you an example that you should do as I have done for you.'"

We are not called to be served, but we are called to serve others. We are called to humble ourselves and push away selfish pride. We are to follow the "Total Package" and lovingly help those God brings into our lives.

I want to share one last story before I let you go. I had the privilege of serving a church in Titusville, Florida, as the Senior High Student Pastor and the Generational Pastor for four years. What a blessing it was to help so many amazing Christian people. God taught me so much as I served at Park Avenue Baptist Church. I also had the privilege to be discipled and mentored by Peter Lord. My brother-in-law, Billy Durham, introduced me to this great man of God. I can honestly say that time with him amazingly changed my life. I thank God regularly for all the wonderful relationships there in Titusville. I could tell you story after story about what God did in my life and the lives of those around me. I don't want to draw this out, so I will jump right in.

THE TOTAL PACKAGE

We had a special guest coming to our church, and I was excited about the opportunity to meet this well-known author. He was well known all over the world for his books. I have read many of them and thought a lot about his writings. I was pumped to meet him, to say the least. The day he was flying into Orlando, Billy came to me and asked if I wanted to go to the airport with him to pick him up. Of course, I was excited to pick up one of my heroes of the faith. We jumped in the car, and it took us about 50 minutes to get to the Orlando airport. I was so excited about meeting this famous author, so, of course, I had to call a couple of my close friends. Wow, what a privilege and honor this was.

We arrived at the airport with a sign with his name. I am not telling you his name because I don't want to bad-mouth anyone or cause harm to his ministry. We recognized his face as he approached us because I had seen it in all his books. He recognized us because we were holding his name on a piece of paper. I was ready to sit down with this man, pick his brain, and have this awesome conversation about God and ministry. I was prepared to soak in his wisdom and learn from this man. His first words to us were, "Here is my luggage." I gladly took his luggage, and we all got in the car and headed to Titusville. He didn't seem to be personal or friendly. He was probably tired from his trip, and I know he had a lot of things on his mind, so no big deal.

Man, this guy was a mover and shaker. He talked on his cell phone all the way to Titusville. Yes, the entire fifty-minute trip. We finally arrived in Titusville at the most excellent restaurant in town. I kept thinking he would put his phone down, at least while we eat and have a conversation. But the calls kept coming, and he only paused to order his meal, and of course, he ordered the most expensive steak on the menu. The meal comes out, and he finally puts his phone down to eat. To my disappointment, I had never sat at the table with such a demanding and rude person. I have never seen someone so full of himself in my entire life.

To tell you the truth, I was a little embarrassed. We left the restaurant and brought the author to his bus, which was waiting at the church. He jumped out of the car and went straight to his bus without saying "thank you" or "it was nice to meet you." To say the least, my bubble was busted. Ten minutes before he was to speak before our church body, Billy and I went to meet him on his bus to take him to the sanctuary. As we approached the sanctuary full of people that were excited about hearing this great author and man of God speak, he flipped a switch and transformed into this super Christian figure. His face lit up, the phone went into his pants pocket, and he was beaming. He was shaking hands and greeting people. He was telling people how good it was to be here. He got up and shared the truth, and the people were encouraged.

I sat there in disbelief. One of my spiritual heroes was a fake. He was a fraud. He was living a lie. He was proud and selfish and had everybody fooled, including me. I never bought another one of his books. As believers in Christ, God calls us to serve people. He calls us to be humble and put others first before ourselves. If you genuinely want to win with people and make a difference in this world, you need to serve others. Today, ask the Lord to reveal what is hindering you. What is it that is hindering you from really serving people? Follow Christ's example and become that "total package" that He encourages us to be. Don't confess to being something you are not.

Chapter 18
The Constant Pursuit

Luke 2:52 And Jesus increased in wisdom and in stature and in favor with God and man.

I am sitting at my dining room table wondering how to close this book out. I wish there were words I could type that would motivate you to give God your all and serve Him with passion forever and ever. I am praying that God will use this book to push you to be that "total package" just like Jesus and to bring a better balance to your life. We all tend to get busy and distracted with life. Then we begin to pull to the left or right. My objective in writing this book is to get you to slow down enough to take an honest look at your life. Be willing to look at each area of your life and see if improvements need to occur. I challenge you to grow in wisdom, to take care of your physical body, to grow in your relationship with God, and to nurture those relationships with those around you.

I am not giving you a four-step process to follow and guaranteeing you a happy life. I am not saying to make all my adjustments, and then you will find contentment and peace. It will look different in each one of your lives. But I am pushing you with love to have some honest and heartfelt conversations with the Lord about what is going on in your life. Talk and tell God about what is going on, and take time to listen to what God is saying back to you.

I will warn you that when we take time to listen to God, He will speak back. Then when He speaks, we are accountable for what the Lord has shown us. In other words, we will have the option to obey God or turn our backs to the Father and run from what He has told us to do. Obedience brings blessings, and disobedience brings punishment. I pray that you will walk in obedience. I pray that you will have the courage to accept what God has placed in front of you and that you will have the courage to make some positive changes in your life.

To close things out, I want to tell you about someone very special to me. His name was Danny Durham. Danny was a couple of years old than me, and we grew up in the same youth group in Albany, Georgia. As a middle schooler, He was everything I wanted to be. Danny was popular, funny, athletic, and a friend to everyone. He was the guy all of us middle school guys admired. Danny went on to sign a football scholarship to Georgia Southern, where he played for Coach Erk Russell and won two National Championships as a player. After his playing days were over, Danny stayed on at Georgia Southern as a Graduate Assistant and collected two more National Championship rings as a coach. That's not bad for a young man from Southwest Georgia. I don't have enough pages to tell you all the things Danny achieved in this life, but I want to cover some highlights.

Danny married Julie Griggs and was the father of three children. Danny took pride in his family; they were the apple of his eye. I could tell you some funny stories about family get-togethers and beach vacations with the Durhams that would have you rolling, but I will contain myself. There was never a dull moment when Danny Durham was anywhere close. He was a great storyteller. Danny would be so caught up in the story that he couldn't sit still. His hands were constantly moving, and he wouldn't sit still. He was very expressive, and he knew how to make everyone laugh.

THE TOTAL PACKAGE

I will never forget that laugh; it was so contagious. When he began to tell a story about old times, everyone stopped what they were doing to listen. He was like a people magnet; he had a charm about him that would make you feel loved and accepted, no matter who you were.

Danny was also a football coach and Athletic Director at a couple of high schools in the state of Georgia. He encouraged and pushed so many young men to be better students and players and to become better people. Being a coach was so much more than a job. It was his calling. He didn't do it for the money, and it was never about building a name for himself; coaching was his ministry. He had a genuine love for his students and players that was unmatched. He was that teacher who never sat down during lunch; instead, he would walk around with his sandwich talking with students. He knew their names, parents, and what they were all about. He loved people, and he invested in their lives. He affected thousands of people.

As I said, Danny was a great athlete in high school and college. He was a decorated football player. But when football was all over, Danny continued to work out and care for his physical body. As a matter of fact, Danny lost some weight and started watching what he ate. He became a very dedicated runner. There was hardly a day that went by that Danny wasn't out, pounding the streets. He would run a couple of miles as if it was nothing to it.

Danny also had a close walk with the Lord and was a man of great faith. He was a leader in his church, sang in the church, and knew God's Word. Danny was also a man of prayer and would pray consistently for his family and friends. He was a well-respected man of God in the community. He was a leader among leaders.

Because of his faith and dedication to the Lord, there was no doubt he asked God for wisdom. There is no way I could tell you how many people and students he helped and encouraged because of his godly wisdom. I can genuinely say Danny was what I called the total package. He constantly pursued wisdom. Danny was a continual learner who surrounded himself with other godly men. He grew in stature and took great care of his body by eating right and working out daily. Danny had a close relationship with the Lord and walked with God daily. He was a man after God's own heart. He dug deep in God's Word and was known to be a man of prayer. Finally, he spent his whole life investing in other people. He reached out to everyone. It didn't matter how smart you were, what social class you come from, or what skin color you had. Danny loved you. He took the time to know your name and wanted to get to know you personally.

With all that, Danny pursued God and did everything he could to live a life that made God smile. But Danny wasn't perfect. He wasn't flawless, but he was close to it. I am sure he had some issues in difficult relationships. Just like many of us, there had to be some challenging days along the way. God never said that living the Christian life was easy. But Danny kept pressing forward and never looked back. He stayed positive and kept cheering others on.

In August 2018, like every other day, Danny took off on his five-mile run. He started at the school and headed for the back gate. Before he could get off campus, Danny collapsed and died from a heart attack. He was only fifty-four years old. Family and friends were shocked and couldn't believe this horrible news. The next day family and friends went to comfort Julie and his kids. Everyone was still in disbelief and numb inside. As we all sat around the kitchen table, the family began to sing and cry together. One of my heroes of the faith had left this earth. To say the least, it was hard to let go of Danny.

A couple of days later, Danny's funeral was held in Columbus, Georgia, in a large church. It all felt like a dream. Was all this happening? All the family gathered in the back of the church, lining up and ready to walk out into the main sanctuary to honor Danny's life. My life was about to change forever. As the sanctuary doors opened and the family began to walk out, I couldn't believe my eyes. The huge sanctuary was full-to-overflowing. Standing room only! Even the overflow room was packed. There wasn't a dry eye there. All these people came to honor a man whom I have always adored. I heard story after story of how Danny encouraged them, how he spoke into their lives, and how he never gave up on them when everyone had turned their backs on them. Danny had made a difference because he invested in the lives of others. Danny loved people just the way that Jesus loved. Yes, he was the total package, just like Jesus.

Danny wasn't perfect, but he strove to pattern his life after Jesus. He constantly pursued the heart of God, and he cared for people. You can say he grew in wisdom, stature, and favor with God and man. Because of that, he invested in eternity and things that would last forever. He made a difference in this world and the world to come. Danny, thank you for giving us all an example of how to live a life that pleases God. Being the total package doesn't make you look good or draw attention to yourself. Instead, it will bring glory and honor to our Lord Jesus Christ and grow His Kingdom.

Philippians 3:10-14: "I want to know Christ and the power of his resurrection and the fellowship of sharing in his sufferings, becoming more like him in his death, and so, somehow, to attain to the resurrection from the dead. Not that I have already obtained all this, or have already been made perfect, but I press on to take hold of that for which Christ Jesus took hold of me. Brothers, I do not consider myself yet to have taken hold of it. But one thing I do: Forgetting what is behind and straining towards what is ahead, I press on toward the goal to win the prize for which God has called me heavenward in Christ Jesus."

Our life is all about the constant pursuit of becoming more like Christ. I have a way to go, but I am hard after it. I am putting my mistakes, shortcomings, and my failures behind me, and I am pressing toward the goal of living a balanced Christ-centered life for His glory.

Now the ball is in your court, and I encourage you to take the time to evaluate your life and see how you measure up in each area of your life. Which area of your life is struggling the most? Don't ignore what God has placed in front of you, and be willing to take the necessary steps to make some improvements. Remember to share with a godly friend what God is calling you to do. We all need that accountability and encouragement. Let's go! Step to the line and take that first step. That constant pursuit of Jesus will take you from just existing to really living.

Colossians 3:17: "Whatever you do, whether in word or deed, do it all in the name of the Lord Jesus, giving thanks to God the Father through him."

Books By Dennis L Taylor

Books are available at Amazon.com

1. Fuel For Today

Dennis L Taylor

About the Author

I started in Student Ministry when I was twenty years old, and it has been my calling for nearly thirty years. My heart was for students to come to know Christ and to grow in their relationship with Him. I love to see God's light bulb fill their eyes and hearts, and I loved sharing the Gospel of Jesus with students who everybody else said were a lost cause. My passion was not only to teach them about a relationship with the Lord but also to give them a real-life example of what it looked like to be walked out in everyday life. My time alone with God has always been my rock, fortress, and high tower. Spending time each morning in prayer, reading God's Word, and taking time to listen to His voice has changed my life forever. I love sharing with young believers who dare to dive deep into the river of God's love. It is so rewarding to invest in the life of other people, watching them go from the shallow end of faith and dive into the deep water of a love relationship with Jesus.

I had the privilege of pastoring two churches, which greatly blessed my family and me. The Lord led us to plant a church in Leesburg, Georgia. It was a time of growth and a time of great joy. I loved preaching God's Word weekly and encouraging and loving families. We started with twelve people in our home one Sunday morning. A short time later, God opened the door to purchase a building on a couple of acres in Lee County. That church is still going strong and is known as Forrester Community Church. I also had the honor to pastor Salem Baptist Church in Worth County, Georgia. Salem is a small country church with a huge heart for God and its community. I was there for a short time, but they have a very special place in my heart.

Today, I serve as the Pastor of Sports and Recreation at Park Avenue in Titusville, Florida. Peter Lord was the founding pastor of Park Avenue Baptist Church. He was also the author of several well-known books such as Hearing God, Soul Care, 959 plan, and many more. He was one of the greatest communicators of God's Word I have ever heard. I had the honor of being discipled by this great man of God back in 2004, as I served as the Senior High Student Pastor. My role today at Park Avenue is to use sports and recreation to reach out to the community around us. As we develop relationships through sports, God provides us an open door to share our Jesus with them and their families. My hope, joy, and calling are to lead as many people as possible into a saving relationship with Jesus. Then encourage them to take those next steps to grow and mature in their faith

www.ingramcontent.com/pod-product-compliance
Lightning Source LLC
Chambersburg PA
CBHW060836050426
42453CB00008B/712